DIMENSIONS
OF THE
QUR'AN

Volume I

by
Sa'dullah Khan

Foreword by Shaykh Seraj Hendricks
Introduction by Dr Maher Hathout

D1378332

Published by:
Multimedia Vera International
434 South Vermont Avenue
Los Angeles, CA 90020

© Copyright 1999
Multimedia Vera International
ISBN. 1–881504–47–6

Cover Design:
Rouzbeh Bahramali

Printed by:
A – 1 Printing & Graphics, Inc.
22873 Lockness Avenue,
Torrance, CA 90501
USA

TABLE OF CONTENTS

i

ii

iv

FOREWORD

In the name of Allah, the most Merciful, the Beneficent

"The best of you are those who study the Qur'an and teach it"
(*Hadith*)

In my long association with Shaykh Sa'dullah Khan – at both
the professional and more casual social levels – I have come to
know him as person with deep commitment to the Qur'an.
This, the casual reader might say, ought to apply to any
Muslim. What distinguishes his commitment, however, is the
fact that it is founded *and* rooted in both a profound love for
the Qur'an and an equally profound understanding of it.
Shaykh Sa'dullah's forthcoming series entitled "The
Dimensions of the Qur'an" will act as sufficient vindication of
his understanding and insights. While his "Dimensions of the
Qur'an" is nothing new to those of us in the Western Cape
(South Africa)– it has been serialized on both Muslim radio
stations and in the *Boorhanool* magazine – its compilation in
serialized book form is a fitting culmination to a remarkable
service rendered by a dynamic scholar of the Qur'an.

His exegesis of the Qur'an stands out in two respects: firstly, a
maturity of approach and secondly, a unique thematic
rendition.

By "maturity of approach" I mean that his work is free from
those awful assumptions of having attained to ultimacy in his
comprehension of the Qur'an, or stated more simply, there are
no pretensions to a monopoly of knowledge in his
interpretations. Anyone schooled in literary traditions,
whether in the Western mould or in the classical Arabic
mould, will know that any text worthy of its name – even in its

v

simplest form of nursery rhymes – can elicit different levels of intellectual and emotional responses which are contingent on the level of engagement of that text in the first place. For us this becomes even more critical when we, as Muslims, engage in interpreting what we regard as the most sacred living text, namely, the Qur'an. Assumptions of monopolies of interpretation – the death-knell of creativity – vis-a-vis the Qur'an, are simply flushed out by the Qur'an itself when Allah (swt) asserts that "*If the ocean were ink wherewith to write the words of my Lord then the ocean would be exhausted before the words of my Lord; even if we added another ocean to it for its aid*" (Q 18:109). The very fact that so many different interpretations have emerged across the ages – since the great beginnings of 'Abdulla ibn 'Abass down to contemporary times – stands as sufficient testimony to this Qur'anic verse. It takes maturity to recognize this simple truth and Shaykh Sa'dullah stands us proud in this regard.

By "unique thematic rendition" I mean that Shaykh Sa'dullah has made accessible and brought to the focus of his audience, in unique conceptual form, those values and meanings which have acted as the primary source of inspiration, not only in the making of the ideal Muslim character and personality, but also in the formation of Islamic culture and civilization.

Finally, I wish to add that while Shaykh Sa'dullah's "Dimensions of the Qur'an" stands out as commendable contribution to our growing literary culture in the Cape, it may also mark an "age of maturation" in that culture.

Shaykh Sa'dullah's work will definitely go much further in raising the standards of our scholarship than the loud and pompous sermonizing which has almost become the daily diet of many a Muslim community throughout the world – communities who are desperately in need of raising themselves above the obscurantist mists of mediocrity and, of course, the stiflingly pedantic.

Shaykh Seraj Hendricks
Azzawia Mosque
Cape Town, South Africa
11 January 1998

بسم الله الرحمان الرحيم

ACKNOWLEDGEMENTS

This book has been written in submission to Allah, as a service to humanity and as *sadaqah jariyah* (perpetual charity) on the soul of my beloved grandmother, Mariam Khan, whose love and care nurtured me. I am grateful to Allah for my respected grandfather, Haji Saleh Khan, who has served as a source of inspiration to me throughout my life.

I would like to extend heartfelt appreciation to my loving parents (Haji Ahmed and Hajjah Fatimah) for their sacrifice and support; and to my uncle, Haji Yaseen Khan, for his consistent motivation.

I express eternal gratitude to all my teachers for sharing their knowledge; to Shaykh Abduraghmaan Alexander for sharing in the presentation of many of the radio programs; and profound thanks to my wife Mariam, sons Ikhlaas and Furqaan, for their patience and unwavering support.

A special thanks to Mu'allimah Fatima Jack, who came all the way from Cape Town to Los Angeles to transcribe and assist in the lay–out of this work.

May Allah reward each according to the best of their deeds.

All praise is due to Allah, salutations and blessings upon the final Messenger, Muhammad, peace be upon him and his family.

ERRATA

Page xi	Line 1	Comprising the highest standard
Page 5	Line 4	as vast as its title
Page 61	Last line	barriers of caste
Page 160	Line 26	wives who fail to
Page 164	Line 3	This word refers to the Being Who comprises all attributes of perfection.

INTRODUCTION

In the Name of Allah, Most Gracious, Most Merciful

One of the many problems that befell the Muslim *Ummah* is the barriers that separated the ordinary Muslim from the Qur'an. Somehow the Muslim person was told in many ways that he or she cannot plug directly to the Qur'an; that they have to go through mediators to receive the Qur'an. The Divine Source of energy and empowerment was actually reduced to ritualism or mere exercise of memorization and melodic recitation. This happened in spite of the Qur'an categorically mentioning that it is a Book of deliverance from darkness to light; a guidance to everyone, that each one is individually responsible and accountable according to their own capacity, to the extent of their understanding and their ability to perform.

A mix up between the intricate technical process of deriving and codifying laws or solving grammatical and linguistic issues; which obviously needs specialization like all branches of knowledge, was mixed up with the availability and the clarity of the message which aims at informing and transforming the individual and society.

The lucid and clear reflections of brother Sa'dullah Khan, his smooth sailing in the oceans of Qur'anic wisdom and beauty is most encouraging and pleasantly inviting the English reader of the Qur'an to plunge again into the ultimate source of enlightenment and empowerment that we have. The eloquence and refreshing intelligent approach of the author renders the topics both exciting and enjoyable.

Dr Maher Hathout
Chairperson of MVI
Los Angeles, CA. USA

AUTHOR'S NOTE

"And We have revealed unto thee the Book as an Exposition of all things; a Guide, a Mercy and as Glad Tidings to those who submit to Allah." (al – Qur'an 16:89)

The Islamic ideology, philosophy and way of life is based on the Holy Qur'an. The historical personality and identity of the *Ummah* (global community of Believers) emanates from and is fashioned by the holy Book. The holy Prophet Muhammad (pbuh) was not only its recipient but also its most authentic expounder, its personification and therefore the greatest exemplar.

The Holy Qur'an is a Book of Guidance, addressing by and large the totality of humanity. Its glorious message is relevant to all people of all times. Its power lies in the fact that it is the Revelation from the Supreme, representing that which is always valid due to its conveyance of the Truth, which by its very nature is perennial. The eternal law thus continues to provide direction for the temporal in all times and climes.

As holy scripture, the distinctive feature of the Qur'an lies in the fact that it affirms and completes the total process of Divine Guidance sent to humanity via revelation. The Holy Qur'an is thus the embodiment of the final most communiqué from the Divine, seeking to reach every level of human understanding through similitudes, parables, reasoning and harkening towards observing natural phenomena and harmonizing with natural law.

The Noble Qur'an, though clothed in human language, is the ultimate ethical code and the primary source of Divine Law.

x

The Qur'an re-affirms all that which is fundamental and relevant in past scripture, compromising the highest standards of reliability, containing lasting commandments, infallible proofs and the criterion (*al – Furqaan*) which serves as the ultimate standard of discriminating between truth and falsehood, good and evil, right and wrong.

When interpreting the Qur'an, one highlights the rationale and wisdom of certain aspects of the Divine text with an effort to convey the relevance of the Qur'anic message to contemporary issues. In this way, *Tafseer* literature reflects Muslim thought and academism at its best for it captures the richness, originality and variety of Islamic contribution to human thought and civilization. Every era has its outstanding contributors, testifying to the inner strength, vitality and relevance of the Qur'anic–cum–Islamic tradition.

However, serious intellectual effort is demanded to respond to the challenging qualitative changes in the contemporary world and the essential human factor is required in comprehending, interpreting and construing from Divine Guidance the most appropriate response for the times. Neither rhetoric nor emotionalism can replace this intellectual responsibility.

In this work, I have selected fourteen extracts from the Glorious Qur'an and elaborated specifically on fundamentals of faith and the theme of social responsibility. I have employed a relatively free interpretative rendering of the text while exercising utmost care and circumspection to safeguard deviation from the literal intent thereof or disturbing the inner coherence of the theme discussed.

The Qur'an is the word of Allah, Allah is Divine and Perfect. Tafseer is the human understanding of the Divine text, human beings are not Divine, *Tafseer* is neither perfect nor final. It is the responsibility of the educated reader to realize this.

May this work serve as some source of understanding, inspiration and motivation, *Insha–Allah*. All praise is due to Allah, all shortcomings are but our own.

S'adullah Khan
Los Angeles, California, USA
Rabi²-ul-Awwal 1420/July 1999

SURAH AL – 'ASR
BY TIME
CHAPTER 103

و العصر
"By the token of time"

Our most valuable capital

This early Makkan revelation takes its title from the opening words "*Wal 'Asr*"; which also constitutes an oath. *'Asr* means *time, era, history, speedy passage of days, succession of ages, afternoon or declining day.*
Allah swears *by the token of time* as witness and as proof of certain contentions. *Time* is a witness to what has passed in human history, witness to life and death, success and failure, rise and fall of individuals and communities. The evidence of Time has been presented for various possible reasons:

i) The Clock of Age is reducing our life by the tick of every passing second. The most valuable capital that we have; Time, is being lost in the process.
ii) Since life is a test of deeds (Q 67:2), the limited, yet fleeting Time is the ambit within which we operate.
iii) To call to mind the events of history.
iv) To emphasize the nearing of the end of human existence on earth.
The holy Prophet (pbuh) is reported to have said:
"Compared to the communities that have passed on before you, life in this world is the same duration as the time between the prayer of 'Asr and Maghrib."
(Bukhari)

1

In a *hadith Qudsi* we are instructed *not to abuse Time.* We are not to accuse Time either; as the great jurist Imam al – Shafi'ie said, *"We blame Time, though we commit the wrongs, Time has no evil except the sins we commit in Time."*

Time is wealth

There is an element of truth in the metaphor "Time is money" (implying that time is valuable). By utilizing time in a meaningful and productive way and through effectively employing our vast potential, much can be achieved. Yet, this metaphor also implies something about the very purpose of life itself; an implication that requires thorough examination. In the Space Age we live in, we have been able to invent things and develop techniques to speed up things and save time. The task that used to take months can be accomplished in minutes; yet there is something ironic about this progress. Despite the proliferation of timesaving devices, life is more hectic than ever before, and no extra time seems to be left for anything meaningful.

We must realize that time is the measure of life, time is a trust (*amaanah*), time is a gift from the Creator and its proper use will determine our outcome for eternity. We should take cognizance of the warning of the Prophet (pbuh) when he said; *"There are two blessings that most delude people, free time and health"* (Bukhari).

We should also seriously reflect on the following Prophetic advice; *"Value five things before five others come to pass: Value Youth before Old Age, Health before Illness, Affluence before Poverty, Leisure before becoming too Busy and value Life before Death"* (Tirmidhi).

2

Every moment that passes by is an opportunity gone, used or abused; never to return. Soon time will be up and we'll have to leave this physical world (Q 3:185).

What happens thereafter will depend on how we used our time that was available to us before that certain but unknown moment of death arrives (Q 18:56). Time is life and our eternal destiny is at stake.

ان الانسان لفى خسر

"Surely humankind is in a state of loss"

We are constantly losing the capital of our existence; minutes, hours, days, months and years. Life is passing on rapidly, not a moment can be retrieved from the stream of the past. Spiritual and material potentialities decline while physical and mental abilities fade. Despite our technological advancements, humanity at large seems nonetheless lost in a quagmire of restlessness, insecurity, uncertainty, hostility, loneliness, stress, faithlessness and disillusionment.

Four principles for salvation

(By the token of time, humanity is in a state of loss)

الا

"Except..."

Once the situation of loss is recognized, we can extricate ourselves from it through the implementation of a universally applicable program that involves the theological, practical, personal, and social doctrines of *Deen al – Islam*.

الذين امنوا

"Those who have Faith" (al – Imaan – Theological Doctrine)

Imaan (Faith) usually forms the basis of conscious activity, since commitment to a cause and the actions that emanate therefrom often reflect a person's belief and thoughts. Actual Faith is inherent in those who are true in thought, word and deed concerning their natural submission to the universal laws that govern the entire cosmos. The submission is not based on mythology, neither on blind acceptance of illogical doctrines, nor on fanatical emotionalism. It is structured on the compliance of the human being to the natural universal laws that govern all existence. *Deen al – Islam* is a Divine system based on reason, Truth, culminating in practical faith, expressed via beneficial action, emanating from sincere intention and manifesting goodwill for all humanity.

و عملوا الصالحات

"Those who do good deeds" – (*Practical Doctrine*)

Righteous and beneficial actions are the worthy products of the fruitful tree of Faith. The term *Saalihaat* is mentioned particularly in the plural form throughout the Holy Qur'an, preceded by the definite article "*al*". This indicates generality, implying the fulfillment of any and all **goods deeds**.

'Amal-us-Saalihaat therefore includes every worthy, pure action that contributes towards individual or social welfare; that can be applied in the way towards soul – perfection, moral improvement; affirmation of justice and alleviation of evil, impurity and oppression.

The Prophet (pbuh) is reported to have said that *Faith and Good Deeds are partners and the one is incomplete without the other.* Faith is thus not a mere thought or belief, free from effect. It changes and orientates the whole entity of a being to its own essence. One cannot escape the "loss" without *Imaan* (possessing True Faith in Divinely revealed, universal Truths) and manifesting *'Amal-us-Saalihaat* (adjusting his / her conduct in harmony with these Truths).

و تواصوا بالحق

"Enjoining Truth" – (*Personal, Conscience – evoking Doctrine*)

The term **Haqq** connotes *truth, reality, that which is verifiable, whatever is based on justice, rights morally incumbent or obligations legally demanded.*
Now for Faith and Goodness to be manifest and evolve in society it must be accompanied by an invitation to that which is Right, Real and True. It is expected of the Faithful to enjoin **Haqq** upon each other. This elicits the Faithful not to only abide by the Truth but also to actively realize their social and moral responsibility by exhorting others to do likewise. Needless to say, the Faithful should be administrators of **Haqq** in their own lives before preaching to and exhorting others.

To bring about a realistic and effective reformation, the all influential environment needs to be changed. Thus, the injunction not only to adopt right and good principles and ideals in themselves, but to convey these to others, thereby creating an atmosphere congenial to the implementation of Faith, Goodness, Justice and Truth.

و تواصوا بالصبر

"Exhorting patient perseverance" – (*Personal and Social Doctrine*)

Sabr means *patience, strength of will, being steadfast amid tribulations, enduring trials and afflictions, constancy despite surrounding changes, forbearance, preparedness to sacrifice, determination in the face of opposition and courage in the face of oppression.*

In our modern lifestyle where anxiety, stress and depression are more common than not, exhortation to ***Sabr*** is indispensable. Allah commands us:

"O you who Believe, seek assistance (and solace) through Patience and Prayer; Surely, Allah is with those who Patiently Persevere. Refer not to those who have been slain in the Path of Allah as being dead; no, they are alive though you perceive it not. Be rest assured that you will be tested with fear, hunger, loss of property, of lives and of fruits of your labor. Convey glad tidings to those who are patient; those who when affliction, trial or tribulation befall them, say: "Surely from Allah we come and unto Him is our return." Such are those on whom the blessings and mercy from Allah descends, such are they who follow the Path of Divine Guidance." (Q 2:153 – 157).

The significance of ***Sabr*** in the Islamic Way of Life can be gauged from the fact that the holy Prophet considered it as *half of Faith* and as *the key to Paradise.*

From 'Asr to Sabr

This surah, constituted of just four verses, is one of the shortest chapters of the Qur'an; but its meaning is as deep and vast its title. It conveys a brilliant source of Guidance; thereby directing individuals, communities, nations and successive generations to the Right Path. We are reminded that a purposeless life without ideals is a waste; that material property, scientific progress and technological advancement can not in themselves save humanity. Salvation lies in having a pure ideology, a practical philosophy, positive action and purposeful lives. The flight of Time provides the testimony that only those who do not waste the opportunity of doing good and being righteous that ultimately reap benefits of existence.

This chapter begins with *'Asr* and ends with *Sabr*; begins with the cyclical experience (Time) and concludes with the expression of constancy (Patience). When the 99 Names of Allah are recited or written, the Name *As – Subur* (the Eternally Constant) is usually the last. Perchance this Divine Attribute is the basis of creation and the element most required for its continued existence.

The four principles for salvation contained in this surah constitute a truly comprehensive program. Such is the significance of this surah, that whenever the companions of the Prophet met they would not leave until they recited Surah al – 'Asr to each other. This, in order to remind each other, and themselves, of the eternal loss that everyone risks if Time is wasted or abused. The great scholar, jurist, swordsman and poet, Imaam Ash – Shafi'e said: *"If Allah were to reveal no other surah besides this surah, it would have sufficed (as complete Guidance) for the Ummah."*

7

THE VERSE OF THE THRONE
(QUR'AN 2:VERSE 256)

الله لا اله الا هو

الحي القيوم

لا تاخذه سنة ولا نوم

له ما فى السموت وما فى الارض

من ذا الذى يشفع عنده الا باذنه

يعلم ما بين ايديهم وما خلفهم

ولا يحيطون بشي ء من علمه الا بما شاء

وسع كرسيه السموت و الارض

ولا يئوده حفظهما

و هو العلى العظيم

Allah, there is no object worthy of worship but Him; the Ever Living, the Self-Subsisting and All-Sustaining. Slumber siezes Him not, nor sleep. Unto Him belongs whatsoever is in the heavens and whatsoever is in the earth. Who can intercede with Him except by His permission? He knows what is before them and what is behind them; and none can encompass any of His Knowledge except what He pleases. His Throne (Knowledge and Authority) extends over the heavens and the earth; and the care of them burdens Him not; and He is the Supreme, the Greatest.

8

This magnificent verse has been named *"Ayat – ul - Kursi"* and has been described as *"The Grand Verse"* in the hadith. It provides, in one piece, unparalleled information about Allah.

الله لا اله الا هو

"Ilah" is an object of worship and **"Allah"** is the title of that Single Absolute Being, in whom is concentrated all attributes of perfection. *"Allah, there is none worthy of worship but Him."* This is the fundamental creed of Islam and the ultimate expression of *Tawhid.* It is an absolute and unreserved negation of any plurality of the Supreme Being. This affirms the unicity and Divine unity of the unbegotten and unbegetting (Q 112:1-4), and confirms the reality that *"Godhead"* in its entirety belongs exclusively to the Eternal Being, Allah.

الحي

This attribute of Allah signifies the Being who is deathless, for *"Al- Hayy"* is on a paradigm denoting perpetuity and thus denotes the **Ever- living.** *"He is the All – Mighty, the All – Wise. Unto Him belong the dominion of the heavens and the earth; it is He who grants life and causes death; and He has power over all things. He is the First (without beginning) and the Last (without ending), He is the Evident and He is the Immanent."* (Q 57:2-3)

القيـوم

Originating from the word *"qaama"* (to stand) it carries by association the connotation of establishing, accomplishing, managing, protecting, having power and authority. *Al – Qayuum* therefore refers to an attribute of Allah that indicates His ability to stand by Himself requiring the support of none, while everything else is in need of His support. He is the unoriginated Who originated everything else. He is the *Self-*

Subsisting and *All-Sustaining* on Whom are dependent all levels of existence.

لا تاخذه سنة ولا نوم

Sinah is derived from *Wasana* which implies slumber, drowsiness, exhaustion, negligence or unguardedness. *Nawm* (Sleep) is the opposite of wakefulness and together *Sinah* and *Nawm* express the opposite of *Qaama*. *"Neither tiredness nor exhaustion overcome Him."*

It is improper for *"Al – Qayyum"* to ever be in a state of *Sinah* or *Nawm*. This is an open refutation of the idea of those who consider the Supreme Being analogous to their own imperfect selves and who therefore ascribe to Him the finite weakness which is characteristic of human beings. In Islam, God is never in need of rest.

له ما فى السموت وما فى الارض

"Unto Him belongs whatsoever is in the heavens and whatsoever is on the earth."

After making reference to the attribute *Al- Qayyum* and negation of any fatigue or slumber on the part of Allah, reference is then made to His ownership. Every conceivable thing is part of creation, part of the universe and thus subject to Allah's authority. The comprehensiveness of Allah's Being *Al – Qayyum* includes ownership of the heavens and the earth with due authority. *"The Beneficent, is established on the Throne. Unto Him belongs whatsoever is in the heavens and whatsoever is on earth; whatever is between them and whatever is below the surface. He is the One to whom you need not call upon aloud for He knows full well whatever is secret and most hidden. He is Allah, there is no deity nor object of worship but He; unto Whom belongs the most beautiful Names and Attributes."* (Q 20:5 – 8)

10

Allah's authority and ownership over creation is such that all their attributes, properties, characteristics and traits exist because of Him. There is no activity connected with anything, from its inception to its ultimate end that does not proceed from the ability and capacity provided by Him.

من ذا الذى يشفع عنده الا باذنه

"Who can intercede with Allah except by His permission,"

Intercession implies being an intermediary in affecting the consequence of a matter. The intercessor thus has some influence on the affair of the matter or thing for which intercession is made. Here, there is an unreserved refutation of the idea that anyone or anything has the power to impose its will on Allah. No one shares independently in Allah's governance of the universe and no one therefore could decisively affect His judgement or decision. Such influence would be contrary to the complete authority and total sovereignty of Allah, unless it is by His design, His decree or His permission.

The Holy Prophet, to whom the Divine Will has been revealed, is the model par excellence for humanity (*Uswatun Hasanah*). The Holy Prophet being the supreme human guide by the design of Allah, leads us to the Path of Salvation and in this sense is *shafi'* (intercessor). He is thus the most appropriate of Allah's creation to be permitted to intercede in the Hereafter.

11

يعلم ما بين ايديهم وما خلفهم
ولا يحيطون بشيء من علمه الا بما شاء

"He knows whatever is before them and whatever is behind them. They cannot comprehend anything of His knowledge except that which He pleases."

The whole tenor of this phrase relates directly to the Omniscience of Allah. Allah's Knowledge is not limited nor measurable for it is not bound by the limitation of the finite. His boundless knowledge is comprehensive, complete and all – embracing; encompassing all dimensions of reality in its entirety. *"And there does not lie concealed from your Lord the weight of an atom in the earth or in heaven; nor anything greater nor anything less."* (Q 10:61) The knowledge that all beside Allah have is acquired by instinct, training and experience. The knowledge possessed by creation is but a study and appreciation of Allah's manifestations which are reflected in His creation.

وسع كرسيه السموت و الارض

"His Kursi extends over the heavens and the earth."

Kursi literally means chair. This word has been variously interpreted by the scholars:
(a) The *Kursi* (chair) and *'Arsh* (throne) of Allah (Q 20:5) is one and the same. The *Kursi* and *'Arsh* is symbolic reference to Divine Sovereignty.
(b) It signifies Allah's power. It is used to connote Divine Authority and relates to Allah's Omnipotence.
(c) It signifies Allah's Knowledge. The word *Kursi* has often been used in Arabic to indicate learning and knowledge. This is evident from the Arabic proverb *"Khayr al- nasi al – karasi"* (the best of people are the learned)

(d) It is an image expressing Allah's Grandeur and Majesty.

There is no doubt that the tenor of this phrase relates to Allah's Omnipotence and All-Encompassing Divine Authority. In cognizance of that, the **Kursi** could be an expression indicating the Divine capacity, originating and maintaining the functioning order which is prevalent in the cosmos.

The Authority and Knowledge of Allah is an indispensable extension of His Divinity, reflected in the maintenance and preservation of everything in the heavens and the earth with all its potentialities, characteristics and variety.

ولا يئوده حفظهما

"And the preservation of both (the heavens and the earth) does not tire Him."

Allah is not burdened by the responsibility of the heavens and the earth, for the management of all affairs is the dominion of Allah. This management is exercised through His knowledge of all existence and His authority over the intermediary causes which He Himself created. Thus, he is not burdened by the preservation of all that which His limitless knowledge and authority encompasses. This is clear indication of Allah's total authority, perfectness of His management, supremacy of His ability, greatness of His sovereignty; His freedom from weakness and imperfection.

و هو العلى العظيم

"And He is the Supreme (Most High), the Greatest."

The ayah concludes by indicating two great principles of Divine Attributes. They reflect Allah's Eminence, Majesty

13

and Grandeur. He is High above all levels of existence, beyond imperfection, beyond comparison and beyond limitations. *He is the Perfect, the Absolute, the Supreme, The Magnificent... the Greatest.*

A'zam – al – Ayah (The Grand Verse)

A person asked the Holy Prophet: "O Messenger of Allah! Which verse in the Book of Allah is the Grandest?" The Holy Prophet (SAW) replied: "*Ayat – ul – Kursi; Allah, there is no deity but Him, the Ever – Living, the Self – Subsisting...*" (*Al – Darin.i*).

The fact that this verse was referred to by a special name indicates the importance attached to it. Its uniqueness is due to the highest nobility of its meanings, the elegance and grace of its style, dealing in detail with the various aspects of monotheism and Divine Authority, establishing the pristine belief of the Absolute Supremacy and Perfection of Allah. Imaam Al – Ghazali (Allah's Mercy be upon him) wrote in his book, *Jawahir – ul – Qur'an; "When you reflect on all the meanings contained in the Verse of the Throne and recite other verses of the Qur'an, you will not find all these meanings of Divine unity, sanctification and explanation of highest attributes combined in a single one of them. This is the reason why the Prophet (pbuh) said that the Verse of the Throne is the chief of the verses of the Qur'an."*

SURAH AL – A'LAA
Allah the Most High
CHAPTER 87

This eighty – seventh chapter in the chronological order of the Glorious Qur'an takes its title from a reference in its opening verse to the attribute of Allah, the *Most High*. This is undoubtedly a Makkan *surah* as is confirmed by the tradition documented in Sahih Bukhari wherein the Sahabi, Bara bin 'Azb, makes reference to the fact that companions such as Mus'ab bin 'Umair and Abdullah ibn Umm Maktum taught Qur'an to the people of Madinah before the arrival of the Holy Prophet (pbuh) there. In that very hadith he states that he had memorized *SURAH AL – A'LAA* before the arrival of the holy Prophet (pbuh) in Madinah from Makkah.

When we analyze the subject matter of this chapter, it has all the distinct traits of a Makkan revelation.

سبح اسم ربك الاعلى

"Glorify the Name of your Cherisher, the Most High"

Litany of praise to Allah

Sabbaha (*glorify/ praise*) is related to *Sabaha* (*swim/ float*). *Ism* (*name*) refers to the word which identifies or specifies the particular from the general. *Rabb* implies Cherisher, Nourisher, Sustainer, Lord and Master, Sovereign, Facilitator of development of inherent aptitudes. *Al A'laa* is a reference to the Absolute Supremacy of the Divine Being. Literally the verse could be translated as *Glorify the most high Name of your Cherisher*, or as *Praise the Name of your Lord, the Supreme*.

The *surah* opens with a command to praise the Creator. The two immediately presented Divine attributes are Lordship (*Rabb*) and Highness (*A'laa*). The attribute "*Highness*" prompts one to look to endless horizons which are afforded to us by the *Rabb* who has endowed us with innate potential to fulfil our true destiny.

The command implies recognizing Allah's Supremacy, acknowledging His Authority, witnessing the manifestation of His reality and remembering His Divine Attributes, while participating with all levels of existence in the free – flowing glorification of *Rabbikal A'laa*.

Tasbeeh

The order to **praise the Name of the Lord, Most High** is given with an air of warmth, amicability and compassion, inspiring one with the splendor of an existence based on constant appreciation of the Divine attributes. After all, everything pure issues from His Essence and despite diversity, their very being is in actual fact an echo of His Reality. The sacred Qur'an testifies; "*Everything glorifies and praises Him, perchance you may not comprehend their Tasbeeh.*" (Q 17:44)

The very rhythm of this *surah*, characterized by the rhyming long vowels with which each of the verses end, creates an aura that imparts a feeling of glorification echoed through the universe.

Since the noble Prophet (pbuh) was the first and direct addressee of the Final Divine Communiqué; he, on account of this particular verse, directed his followers *to recite SUBHANA RABBI AL A'LAA (Glorified is my Lord, the Most High) in the prostration of every prayer*, as if this recitation is

16

in compliance with the command given in this verse. (Abu Dawud)

It should be noted that the most important *Dhikr* in the prayer is *SUBHANA RABI AL A'LAA* which is constantly and consistently repeated when one assumes the humblest position, *Sajdah* (Prostration). This state of utmost humility combines with the ultimate state of permanent love which is expressed through constant conscious glorification.
"Certainly, the Dhikr (Remembrance) of Allah is the greatest (pre- occupation)" (Q 29:45).

الذى خلق فسوى والذى قدر فهدى
"(Allah, the Glorified and Most High) – Creates, Fashions proportionately, Imbues with appropriate ability and Provides (the ultimate) Guidance."

Process of Divine Creativity

The litany of Praise to Allah continues with direct reference to the process of Divine Creative Activity which is manifested in four graded stages:
Takhleeq – Allah brings into existence the previously non – existent.
Taswiyah – Fashioning the created with due proportion and in a form ideal to its level of existence.
Taqdir – Assigning to the Creation an appropriate role and imbuing it with ability consistent with its form.
Hidaayah – Granting each level of creation internal and external modes of information which serves as guidance for natural interaction and meaningful co-existence.

This entire process of Divine Creative Activity is an

17

expression of the Divine Lordship (*Rububiyah*) of the Most High (*AL A'LAA*).

Creation and proportion

Glorification of the Most High is inspired by observing the wonders of creation and in acknowledging the Divine Creative Genius Who originated all existence (Q 2:117). It should be born in mind that appreciation of creation; and through it the acknowledgment of the Majesty of the Creator, will be proportionate to the individual's awareness and comprehension of the wonders of creation (Q 3:190 – 191).

The workings of nature indicate that creation is collectively co-ordinated so that each may appropriately perform its particular role. This perfect balance in collective excellence is easily observable in every one of the numerous kinds of creation; from the calculated structure of the minute atom, through the detail of the grooves on each fingertip, to the systemic co–ordination of the mind–boggling galaxies. Certainly, there must be a creator who created with due proportion and fashioned with ever – fashionable design. This we are bound to acknowledge, despite the fact that our scientific appreciation of existence covers only a scanty part of the visible and tangible world, beyond which surely extends an ever expanding universe of which we comprehend only to the level befitting our limited capacity.

Taqdir and *Hidaayah*

The entire cosmos operates in accordance with the dictates of the universal law of nature, which in turn, is the effect of Divine Will (Q 30:30) in operation. Since the world of creation is sustained by definite laws (*taqdir*) governing the potential of each category of creation, these laws are in harmony with one another and are the evidential base of all systemic analyses and scientific advancement.

By '*taqdir*' is implied that each object of creation is made subject to the laws intrinsic to its nature in order that it may have the capacity to fulfil its function. Whenever the Holy Qur'an asserts that nothing happens against the 'Will of God', it pertains to the inherent potentialities of each creation and the natural laws by which it is circumscribed (Q 4:72 – 73; 3:165). Even as a human being conforms to the physical laws of nature for a life of order, so is he instructed to obey Divine Guidance for wordly peace and bliss.

i) **Freedom of will**

The human being is the architect of his own destiny and the passing vicissitudes of life provide the material with which to design his future.

There is no compulsion on the part of the Creator brought to bear on a person to adopt any particular course of action (Q34:40 – 42; 35:18; 73:19; 76:29 – 31). Allah has simply pointed out the best course. Whether that course be followed or not is the choice left to the individual whose prerogative it remains, "*Verily, We have shown the human being the Right Path; he may be grateful and give thanks or be ungrateful and disbelieve*" (Q 76:3)

The Qur'anic verdict on freedom of will is abundantly clear. It has positively declared the human being's undisputed right to make a decisive choice between good and evil, right and wrong. This point has been repeatedly emphasized to clearly convey the idea of human choice, lest man forgets the responsibility emanating from his personal conduct. As a matter of fact, the entire trend of Qur'anic ethics points in this direction; *"Say, the truth is from your Lord, whosoever wishes may choose to believe and whosoever wishes may choose to disbelieve"* (Q 18:29 – 31). Of course, each will have to bear the positive or negative consequences of their choice.

In keeping with the spirit of the Qur'anic verse (53:59) *"Man shall have nothing except what he strives for"*, the great poet – philosopher of Islam, 'Allama Dr. Muhammad Iqbal said; *"It is by our willfully executed actions that we attain success in this life and earn paradise or hell – fire in the Hereafter. In the essence of our being, we are neither pre-destined to paradise nor the fire."*

ii) **Divine gift of guidance**

The Holy Qur'an states that *Hidaayah* is a Divine Gift; *"Our Provider is He Who has granted everything its particular nature then provided it with appropriate guidance."* (Q 20:50)

Hidaayah is common to all creation and each category has its own level of consciousness; whether it be instinctive and intuitive or sensory and intellectual. However the ultimate guidance is that vouchsafed to humanity via the agency of Prophets and is termed Divine Guidance; *"We have created human beings from the union of sexes, granted him sensory faculties and provide the Ultimate Guidance to the Right Path; whether man be grateful or not"* (Q 76:2-3). Therefore we are instructed: *"Say! Certainly the Guidance of Allah is the Ultimate Guidance"* (Q 6:71).

20

Reasons for *Tasbeeh*

The first three verses of this *surah* gives various reasons for the remembrance and glorification of Allah...

- Allah has brought us into being
- Allah has endowed us with the faculties and capacities that are essential for our physical, intellectual and spiritual development
- Allah has proportioned the whole scheme of existence in a manner conducive to goal – orientated development
- Allah has determined (not pre – destined) the scope and also circumscribed the parameters of our potentialities, consistent with our faculties and capacities
- Allah has revealed Guidance for the fulfillment of the objective and purpose of human existence.

These verses inspire one with the splendor of life, of an existence based on constant appreciation of the Divine; thus do we glorify Him...
"All glory to Allah, the Lord of Power and Honor, Whose Grandeur extends far beyond any approximation. Peace be on all His emissaries. All forms of praise due to Allah, the Lord of all existence" (Q 37:180-182).

والذى اخرج المرعى فجعله غثاء احوى

"And He causes the pasturage to emerge and then causes it to become dark stubble."

Reality of mortality

Making reference to birth, growth, fulfillment of purpose and eventual decay of living things; the example of vegetation is used. Vegetation is the most abundant of living things and is the base of the natural food chain.

Plants are symbolic of the reality of mortality. When plants are in growth they produce nutrition through the process of photosynthesis; when dry, it is useful for grazing animals and as fuel for fire; and when it decays it is ideal fertilizer for cultivable lands. The vegetation drying and darkening could also be a reference to the formation of underground minerals such as coal, so useful for industry. Thus vegetation is useful in every stage and serves a purpose according to the elaborate planning of the *Glorified One Who Creates, Proportions, Determines and Guides*.

There is also an implicit connotation that plants are harvested, utilized and ultimately expended. Similarly, *every living thing must eventually come to its appointed end* (Q 3:185); yet, *you prefer this temporary life, while the life to come is better and everlasting* (Q 87:16 – 17).

سنقرئك فلا تنسى الا ما شاء الله

"We shall cause you to recite so that you shall not forget, except what Allah wills…"

Rehearsing and retaining Divine Guidance

The holy Prophet being human, and as such, was apt to forget issues pertaining to the affairs of daily life. However, Allah in

22

His infallible wisdom has so gifted the unlettered Prophet that revelation received by him remained so indelibly imprinted in his mind and on his heart that he was never found to forget or falter in reciting revealed portions.

It is not plausible that the One Who revealed the Qur'an to the Prophet should cause him to forget anything of it. After all, the Qur'an being the Final Divine Communiqué, has been assured Divine Protection against distortion, interpolation or loss. The promise of protection has been given in most emphatic terms: *"Verily, We have revealed the Reminder and We shall certainly be its Protector."* (Q 15:10)

The reference to forgetting is probably in relation to:

i.) The elements of cumulative knowledge which humankind acquire through the ages and collectively "remember", but forget, discard or abandon whatever becomes redundant due to passage of time or due to the acquisition of more advanced and comprehensive information.

ii.) The abrogated message of previous Prophets is "caused to be forgotten" or superceded by the Final Revelation (Q 2:105 – 107).

iii.) Due to the oral nature of Qur'anic revelation, the recitation aids memory, assisting the Prophet not to forget it, though insignificant issues are otherwise forgotten.

This also highlights the distinction between Allah's Intrinsic Knowledge and the Prophet's gifted knowledge.

انه يعلم الجهر وما يخفى

"… Surely He Knows the apparent and the hidden."

23

Beyond physical limitations

Due to His Supreme and Manifest (*Zaahir*) nature, Allah has the information of and power over all things. His Hidden (*Baatin*) attribute signifies His ability to comprehend the humanly incomprehensible.

These Divine attributes confirm that Allah is beyond the limitations of time and space. He Who is above constraints informs the Prophet about whatever is necessary for guiding human beings via revelation. In that process, nothing overt or covert is overlooked.

و نيسرك لليسرى

"And We shall smooth your way to ease."

System of ease

This verse could be a reference to:
i.)   The fact that the Qur'anic teachings are so comprehensive as to meet the exigencies of changing times and situations without difficulty;
ii.)   That the Qur'anic injunctions are simple to understand and easy to implement;
iii.) The ease with which the Qur'an could be memorized;
iv.)   That the future would eventually be easier than the past.

This verse is furthermore a statement about the general tendency of ease inherent in the System of Islam. It reiterates the link between the nature of Islam, the practice of the Prophet and the tendency of the natural world. We live in a

24

universe that operates harmoniously and has the basic feature of being in a state of ease. Hence, the Messenger and the Message (Q 5:6) share this basic feature with the existing natural order. Allah describes the Message as: *"We have made the Qur'an easy to understand and implement, are there any who reflect and pay heed."* (Q 54:22). *Allah lays no hardship in the observance of the Deen* (Q 2:286). Taking into consideration the limitation of human ability, Islam imposes no burden beyond human capacity. The *Ummah* of Islam is expected therefore to evolve as a median nation, *Ummatan wasata* (Q 2:143); as lenient and easy–natured as its guide (Q 3:159).

The holy Prophet (pbuh) is reported to have said that *"this Deen (System of Islam) is of and easy nature. Anyone who pulls hard against it shall be the loser."* (Bukhari) *"Make matters easy not difficult"* (Muslim and Bukhari). He also advised that *"a rider riding hard neither reaches his destination nor keeps his transport"* (Bukhari). The Holy Qur'an describes the Prophet himself as a source of *"mercy to humanity"* (Q 21:107), who has come *"to relieve people of their burdens"* (Q 7:157). It was he who instructed: *"What I command you to do, do to the best of your ability"* (Bukhari).

Keeping all this in mind we appreciate the description of a Believer in the words of the Best of Believers (pbuh): *"A Believer gets on well with others and is easy to get along with"* (Al – Daraqutni).

Being mindful of the Reminder
After referring to revelation and Allah's promise of success for the Prophet's mission, his greatest duty is mentioned thus:

فذكر ان نفعت الذكرى

"So remind, for surely reminding does benefit"

There is not a single spiritual duty commanded by the Qur'an which is not accompanied by an appeal to reason, to meditate, to reflect or to ponder. Once the Prophet has conveyed his message, everyone is left to choose his/her way.

"Whosoever chooses to be guided does so to his own benefit and whosoever chooses to go astray does so to his own detriment ."(Q 17:15)

سيذ كر من يخشى
و يتجنبها الاشقى الذى يصلى النار الكبرى
ثم لا يموت فيها ولا يحيى

While admonishing and reminding, it is mentioned what kind of people will benefit from the Reminder and what kind would abstain, and what would be the consequences of the choice of either of them; *"The Reminder will be received by those who fear (the consequences of their evil), but will be avoided by the wretched; they will enter the great fire, neither dying therein nor living."*

Those who truly receive and reflect on it are the humble, sincere acknowledgers of Truth, who turn to Allah in humility and are overawed by His Majesty. If human beings however, do not heed the message, they will live in a void, uninspired by the reflections of reality that surround them; turning a blind eye, a deaf ear, a cold heart and senseless mind to the evidence manifested.

Though Allah has bestowed upon human beings faculties of observation, hearing and reasoning, some people do not use it properly. Thus, because of their own failings and heedlessness, they suffer the worst consequence; *"And certainly destined for hell are many among jinn and human beings who have hearts (and conscience) with which they fail to understand; eyes with which they fail to see; and ears with which they fail to hear. They are like beasts of burden – in fact, even more astray. Such are the utterly heedless."* (Q 7:179)

The "Great Fire" is reference to the final penalty in the Hereafter in contrast with the minor penalties of this world. The damnation is such that there is no real "life" in hell, for real life is only for the righteous; neither is there death, because death signifies a state of complete rest.

Pre-requisite for success

قد افلح من تزكى و ذكراسم ربه فصلى

"Successful indeed is he who purifies himself, glorifies the Name of his Lord and establishes prayer."

Purification here is used in the widest sense of the word as success is guaranteed at the highest level.

Falaah (Success)

The characteristics of the successful ones are detailed in Chapter 23 Verse 1-12 as ... *Believers who turn to Allah in humility through conscious prayer; avoid vain and futile behavior; engage themselves in pursuits that purify them while availing their time, efforts and abilities in the cause of goodness; guarding their chastity; discharging their obligations and fulfilling their responsibilities; are in constant communion with Allah and never estranged from His awareness.*

In *Surah al-A'laa* the pre-requisites for *Falaah* (Success) are broadly categorized as:
i) *Tazkiyah - (Spiritual growth and purification)*
ii) *Dhikr - (Constant consciousness of the Divine)*
iii) *Salaah - (Prayer)*

Falaah (ultimate success, or prosperity in the highest sense) is for those who purify themselves (spiritually, mentally) and remember, glorify (and meditate on the Name of) the Supreme (to enhance spirituality), and enjoin prayer (for His remembrance).

i) Tazkiyah (Purification)

Linguistically, the root of this term denotes cleansing and development. The ideology conveyed by Prophet Muhammad (pbuh) is the fulfillment of the supplication of Prophet Ibrahim (A.S.) as documented in the holy Qur'an; *"Our Lord! Send among them an Apostle of their own, who shall rehearse Your signs to them and instruct them in al-Kitab (the Holy Qur'an) and al-Hikmah (wisdom), and yuzakeehim (purify them), for You are the Exalted in Might, the Wise.* (Qur'an 2:129)
This verse intimates Prophet Muhammad's mission to be the establishment of three major institutions; *al-kitab* (the Holy Qur'an as a source of Guidance), *al-hikmah* (wisdom – the exercise of one's discerning faculty to acknowledge,

appreciate and implement what is best) and *al-tazkiyah* (spiritual purification which manifests itself through moral rectitude and righteous conduct). From this we deduce that a true believer is one who attains knowledge of the Qur'an, implements it while constantly purifying his heart and soul.

Tazkiyah – tun – Nafs refers to the purification of the inner self from the evils of bad intention, deceit, hypocrisy, treachery, carelessness, selfishness, cowardice, thoughtlessness and arrogance.

Tazkiyah (purification or growth) also implies developing the self from the lowest stage to the highest level; from the *Nafs al – 'Ammarah* (lowest level, where one acts without conscience), through *Nafs al – Lawwamah* (intermediate level, where the conscience awakens in one a sense of guilt and regret for wrongful behavior, and an effort is made for rectification and restitution), to *Nafs ul – Mutma 'innah* (the contented soul, pleased by that which pleases Allah and never deviating from the Path of goodness and righteousness).

The individual has to traverse various stages (*maqaamaat*) of spiritual stations to attain progress toward Godliness and spiritual purity; *tawbah* (sincere repentance), *muhasabah* (constant critical self – examination), *wara'* (avoiding evil), *ikhlaas* (sincerity of intention), *khudu'* (humility), *hayaa'* (implementation of modesty and developing a higher sense of shame), *ju' wa tarak – ush – shahwah* (abstention from submitting to the hunger of passion and desires), *mahabbah* (develop love for that which Allah loves), *sakhaa* (selfless generosity). This must result in *khuluq – un – hasan* (excellent character with ideal behavior).

In *Surah al-Shams* (Ch.91) Allah swears seven oaths to

emphasize the culminating promise of ultimate success for those who exercise *Tazkiyah*...

"...*Truly successful is he who purifies his self (nafs), debased is he who corrupts his self*" (Q 91:9-10)

ii) Dhikr (Remembrance of Allah)

The more we reflect on the grand design of the universe, the more we are reminded of the Designer. How many forces must come together with perfect co-ordination before a seed can sprout? What keeps this immensely complex universe working so flawlessly, from the simplest to the most complex things? There are indeed pointers to the Creator in every atom of everything in this universe; "*In the creation of the heavens and the earth, and the alternation of night and day, there are indeed Signs for people of understanding – people who remember Allah, standing, sitting and lying down.*" (Q 3:190-191). This remembrance (*dhikr*) is indeed itself a source of strength for the Believer.

The Qur'an undoubtedly emphasizes the need for *Dhikr*; "*O Believers! Remember Allah with much remembrance and glorify Him early and late*" (Q 23:41). The Qur'an itself is referred to as al-Dhikr (The Remembrance) in (Q 15:9). Allah furthermore states; "*We have made the Qur'an easy to remember (and an easy mode of remembrance), are there any who care?*" (Q 54:17).

To pronounce words reflecting the attributes or glory of Allah is *Dhikr* by tongue. To understand and reflect on Allah's Majesty is *Dhikr* by heart. Both these desirable modes of remembrance reinforce each other; so conscious oral repetition engraves the words in the heart while understanding and reflection gives meaning and life to the spoken word.

30

Together they assist us in focussing on our destination while journeying through life in this world. All forms of *Dhikr* help us develop and reinforce our relationship with the Divine. *"Keep in remembrance the Name of the Lord and sincerely devote yourself whole-heartedly to Him."* (Q 73:8) The holy Prophet reported that Allah informs: *"I am with the thought of My servant and Am with him when he remembers Me. If he remembers Me in his heart, I too remember him in My heart. If he remembers Me in an assembly, I too recollect him in an assembly, and this assembly is better than his assembly"* (Bukhari).

Furthermore, forgiveness and reward are promised to those men and woman who remember God: *"... and men who remember Allah much, and woman who remember Allah much – for such has Allah prepared forgiveness and immense reward."* (Q 33:36) The great spiritual luminary, Hasan al-Basri (may Allah have mercy on his soul), commenting on the above verse said: *"You should seek joy in three things; performance of prayer, remembrance of Allah and the Qur'an."* This statement is in keeping with what the Prophet, upon whom be peace, said: *"These hearts are subject to corrosion; to polish them, one should regularly read the Qur'an, remember death and join the circles of dhikr."*

Dhikr is the companion and spirit of actions. See how Allah has paired it with *Salaah,* which is the best of all acts of worship, and made *Dhikr* the very reason for it, when He says, *"Establish Salaah (Prayer) for my Dhikr (Remembrance)"* (Q 20:14).

Obligations like prayer and pilgrimage are the means to accomplish *Dhikr – ullah* as Allah ordained; *"And proclaim the pilgrimage among people; they will come to you on foot and (mounted) on every means of transport, journeying through deep and distant mountain highways, so that they may witness the benefits (provided) for them, celebrating and remembering the Name of Allah through the days appointed"* (Q 22:27-28).

And at the end of *Surah al-Fajr* (89:29-30), Allah conveys what is said as He receives the successful ones at death: *"O soul in the state of being mutma'innah, (O tranquil soul or O human being who has attained to inner peace), Return to your Lord and Sustainer, well pleased and pleasing (Him). Enter then, together with My true servants; yes, enter My Paradise."* The word *mutma'innah* occurs in related forms in thirteen places in the Qur'an. The noun from this word is *tuma'neenah*. *Tuma'neenah* means calmness, serenity, peacefulness and tranquility. It signifies a state of composure and equanimity. It implies a feeling of total security, of having complete peace of mind, being at ease with oneself; a state so sought after yet rarely experienced in this age. That pleasant and noble state of the heart is attained through Remembrance of Allah, *"Those who believe and whose heart find satisfaction in Dhikr – ullah (the Remembrance of Allah), such find contentment"* (Q 13:28).

iii) *Salaah (Prayer)*

Pillar of Faith

Salaah is a pillar of Islam and its performance at prescribed times is an obligatory duty upon every mature, mentally sound Believer. It is a manifestation of obedience in practice and an expression and symbol of one's faith. The holy Prophet (pbuh) is reported to have said that *"Salaah is the core of 'Ibaadah* (servitude to Allah)" and that *"the best 'Ibaadah is Salaah."* (Mustadrak al – Hakim)

Prayer in history

All Messengers of Allah from Adam to Muhammad (peace be upon all of them) were commanded to establish the institution of prayer. This is evident from numerous verses in the holy Qur'an: Abraham (pbuh) (Q 14:37-40); Isaac and Jacob (pbut) (Q 21:73); Moses (pbuh) (Q 20:11-14); Zacharia (pbuh) (Q 3:39); Mary (pbuh) the mother of Prophet Jesus (Q 3:43); Jesus ('Isa – pbuh) (Q 19:30-31).

The Prophet Muhammad (pbuh) experienced the highest manifestation of the Glory of Allah on the Night of the *Mi'raj* (ascension). He experienced great joy and contentment in communion with God; there he was given the gift of prayer and the news that if Muslims observe the institution of prayer, they will enjoy the pleasure and satisfaction of being in communion with Allah. Muhammad (pbuh) therefore said: *"Prayer is the Mi'raj of the Believer."*

Importance of Salaah

The holy Prophet (pbuh) acknowledged time and again the importance of *Salaah* and referred to it as *a pillar of Islam* and *the first matter a person would be questioned about on the Day of Reckoning.* Even on his deathbed, he urged his followers to *safeguard the institution of prayer.*

As a cardinal institution of Islam, *Salaah* reflects its religious, spiritual, moral, social, cultural and political objectives. Centers established for congregational prayer (Mosques / *Masajid*) serve as the axis for the *Ummah* (global community of Believers). *Salaah* is the binding force between Believers; whosoever deliberately breaches this bond by abandoning *Salaah*, borders on a state of unbelief.

It is evident that *Salaah* is the foremost link between the Believer and Allah. It keeps alive one's relationship with Allah and ever-conscious of Godliness. It is an expression of supra–national unity which is one of the greatest social ideals of Islam. It induces in Believers a spirit of universal brotherhood and sisterhood.

Salaah is a constant reminder to the Believers that they are brethren in Faith, who are to remain united as a single people, otherwise they will fall into disputes through which will depart their power and their unity will be shattered; *"And obey Allah and His Messenger; and fall not into disputes, lest you lose heart and your power depart; rather be patient and persevering"* (Q 8:46).

Prayer as a force for unification and a source for solidarity

When Muslims perform *Salaah*, they pray in the same manner, same prescribed times, face the same *qiblah* and pray in the same language. Prayer is thus a great force for unification of Muslims worldwide. The uniformity in prayer strengthens universal brotherhood and helps in the realization that all Muslims are one fraternity.

Punctuality

Allah commands, *"Establish regular prayer; for prayer is enjoined at prescribed times"* (Q 4:103). The consistent performance of prayer at stated times, is a training in punctuality and teaches the worshiper the appreciation of time.

Humility

Regular prayer brings about consciousness of the insignificance of the individual creation before the Grandeur

34

and Majesty of the Creator. Humility thus becomes engraved in the psyche of the conscientious worshiper. Such are promised success; *"Surely those believers attain success, who humble themselves in their prayer."* (Q 23:1-2)

Self – development and moral development

Prayer implies a degree of self-discipline in the individual. There exists no restraint from evil better than consistent and conscientious prayer. The Qur'an refers to this, *"Establish regular prayer, for it restrains from shameful activity and unjust deeds."* (Q 29:45)

Prayer develops qualities of patience, endurance and contentment; qualities which are essential in the service of justice, equity and goodness and serve as a source of strength in the face of trials and tribulations of life. The believers are directed to seek Allah's help through prayer: *"O you who believe. Seek help with patient, perseverance and prayer; for God is with those who patiently persevere."* (Q 2:153) Prayer, on every performance, strengthens one's will power and reaffirm one's trust in Allah, while developing the individual emotionally, spiritually and mentally.

Purification

Wudu (ablution) is essential before every prayer as Allah commands in (Q 5:7). The Messenger of Allah said, *"The key to Paradise is prayer, and the key to prayer is purity."*

Ablution removes physical dirt as prayer wipes out spiritual pollution. *"Surely, Allah loves those who turn to Him and those who (physically and spiritually) purify themselves"* (Q 2:222). Ablution is thus a preface to spiritual rejuvenation and moral regeneration, a key to the key – hole of the eternal door of success.

Dimensions of prayer

In the holy Qur'an we are commanded strictly to guard the institution of *Salaah* (Ch 2:v 238) for the guarding of prayer is not simply the observance of the exterior physical form; it is both the form and the spirit to which attention is drawn; both the outer and the inner dimensions. In that very same verse we are commanded to stand up in true obedience to Allah. This aims at generating the spirit of humility in relation to the Divine. Very often the external behavior of a person serves as an index to inner devotion or feeling towards the Supreme. The Qur'an reprimands those who merely observe the outward form of *Salaah* but do not conform to its spirit. In Chapter 107 Allah says: *"Shame to those worshippers who are unmindful of their prayers."* These verses indicate that worship does not consist merely of physical rituals. Undoubtedly there is an outward form of *Salaah* which is an essential part, but the outward form must be accompanied by consciousness and the earnest desire to submit to the commands of Allah in word, form and deed. *Salaah* is in actual fact a manifestation of that commitment.

A true Believer feels *Khushu'* and *Khudhu'* in the Prayer due to an increased awareness of the presence of Allah. *Khushu'* is a condition of the heart and the mind which results in constant consciousness of the Supreme Being. *Khudhu'* is the effect of this consciousness on the physical self which is manifested by submission and humility. *"Believers are those who when Allah is mentioned, feel a tremor in their hearts, and when they hear His Signs being rehearsed find that their Faith strengthened... They are of those who establish regular*

36

prayer." (Q 8: 2-3) *Salaah* is in fact a constant reminder of the reality of human servitude to Allah. Prayer provides opportunities for harmonious functioning of the outer and the inner dimensions of the human being in order to achieve Divine enlightenment. The ideal balance between the outer and the inner; the physical, mental and spiritual, in *Salaah*, assists human beings to achieve true communion with the Creator.

Salaah is the symbol of Faith

Salaah is obedience in practice (Q 21:73) and truly a symbol of one's faith (Q 22:41). Allah promises; "*The Believers must eventually win through; those who humble themselves in prayer... and who strictly guard the institution of prayer.*" (Q 23:1 – 12)

بل تؤثرون الحيوة الدنيا و الاخرة خير وابقى

"*But you prefer the life of this world, although the Hereafter is better and everlasting.*"

Having sketched the two different ends of the deviant and the pious, this *surah* brings to attention the main reason for the failure which lead the wretched headlong into the great fire; "***Yet you prefer this present life while the life to come is better and longer lasting***". The short – sighted preference for this temporary, mundane life is the primary reason for most of the misery which befall many human beings. It is the materialism of this world that blinds man from taking heed of the warning given to him by Prophets throughout history.

The Qur'an refers to the present life as "*Dunya*", which connotes *contemptuousness, temporary* and *ease of access.*

37

The after – life is better in quality and duration. The holy Prophet peace be upon him is reported to have said, *"This world is the abode for one who has no real abode. Those who indulge only in the pursuit of worldly gains are indeed foolish."* It is clear that only the foolish ones deprived of sound judgment, would prefer the short and the temporary over the eternal. The holy Qur'an too criticizes the attitude of those who prefer the worldly life to the life of the Hereafter, those who prefer the fleeting to the everlasting; *"Are you pleased with the life of this world rather than the Hereafter?" But little is the enjoyment of this world in comparison to the Hereafter."* (Q 9:38)

ان هذا لفى الصحف الاولى

صحف ابراهيم و موسى

"Surely this is in the former scriptures, including the scriptures of Abraham and Moses."

It must be realized that the preference of the good of the Hereafter to the transitory attraction of this life is a fact and a great truth which has been conveyed to human beings by Prophets throughout history.

In these verses we are reminded that the essential principles are common to all and these were preached by all those who were emissaries of Allah. The basics of those universal values which were outlined in the ancient scriptures of Abraham and Moses are the same which are manifested in this final Revelation, the Qur'an. The Truth is one and the source of Truth is One, therefore Faith is one. All teachers of Truth throughout history taught the same Truth, for the Origin is one. The reference to the scriptures of Abraham and Moses are only given as examples of earlier receptions and transmissions of Divine Revelations, thus stressing the two – fold fact of continuity in the human being's religious experience and identifying the fact that the basic Truths preached by all Prophets emanate from One Divine Source.

The Creator, the best of creation and the best of guides

This *surah* is constituted of three parts.
Part one (from verse 1 – 13) contains instructions regarding the praise of Allah, reference to the Attributes of Allah and Majesty of the Supreme Being.
The second portion deals with the response of human beings to Divine Revelation and their submission or non-submission to the Truth. Verses 14 – 17 express concisely the causes for the felicity of the Believers and the failure of the wicked. In addition, it imparts clear indication of the easy nature of Islam, of the Messenger and the Mission which he fulfilled.
The last portion of the *surah*, (verses 18 – 19) reiterate the two fold fact of continuity in human religious experiences and of the identity and uniformity of the basic truths and universal values preached by all Prophets (pbut). This Qur'an is thus a verification of past scripture.

When we reflect upon the contents of this *surah*, we realize that it comprehensively includes Islamic concepts and guidance for human existence. It incorporates the Supremacy of Allah, the reality of Divine communication and the inevitability of retribution. It affirms the basic principals of established truths.

The most beloved companion of the Prophet and his son-in-law, *Sayyidena* Ali (may Allah ennoble his countenance) reports that *the holy Prophet especially loved this surah*. Historic evidence indicates this *surah* to be the first one recited by Muslim immigrants to the people of Madinah. The famous traditionist, Imam Muslim, transmitted a report that the *Prophet used to read this surah together with the surah that follows it (Chapter 88) in the Eid prayers and in the Friday prayers.* When pondering over the message of this *surah*, it is little wonder that it was so dearly loved by the holy Prophet.

SURAH AL – MU'MINUN
CHAPTER 23: VERSES 1 – 16

This *surah* derives its title from reference to the Believers (*Mu'minun*) in its opening verse. The entire *surah* was revealed during the middle stage of the Prophet's residence at Makkah and at the climax of famine in that region.

Characteristics of Believers

قد افلح المؤمنون

"Successful indeed are the Believers."

With this verse begins the description and identification of the true Believers and the conditions or prerequisites to be fulfilled by Believers in order to attain the ultimate success. The first condition is that of Faith, for it binds one to an ideology and philosophy of life based on Divine Guidance.

الذين هم فى صلاتهم خشعون

"Those who humble themselves in prayer."

After Faith, there is immediate reference to *Salaah* which is a physical manifestation of willful obedience to the Divine. Prayer is a pillar of Faith and an expression and symbol of Belief. *Khushu'* is a spiritual condition which emanates from within the psyche and the consciousness of the worshipper, making him ever aware of the grandeur and majesty of the Supreme Being.

و الذين هم عن اللغو معرضون

"And those who avoid what is vain."

41

The avoidance of idle and futile actions is a natural and inevitable consequence of humility in prayer. It is indeed a trademark of the Believer to avoid that which is nonsensical, futile and false. *"Believers are those who bear no false witness and who pass by anything vain with honorable avoidance."* (Q 19:74)

و الذين هم للزكاة فاعلون

"Those who (actively purify themselves and) pay the Zakah."

It is the nature of true Believers to selflessly spend their wealth or expend of their time and skills (which Allah has endowed them with) in the cause of goodness. *Zakah* denotes cleansing and development. It is part of the spiritual progression of the Believer to be of those who cleanse themselves externally and (more specifically) internally; as well as to cleanse their lawful income through charity. It must be remembered that the objective of *Zakah*; besides being provision for the relief of the distressed and promotion of economic welfare, is also to discourage the hoarding of money. The cleansing, therefore, is both a spiritual and physical exercise.

و الذين هم لفروجهم حافظون
الا على ازواجهم او ما ملكت ايمانهم
فانهم غير ملومين
فمن ابتغى وراء ذالك فاولئك هم العادون

"And those who guard their chastity except from their wives or what their right hand possesses, for then they are not to be blamed."

History bears testimony to the ruin of those who indulged in immorality and therefore the guarding of chastity is considered a most sacred duty.

The term *malakat aymanuhum* has often been misconstrued to imply that Muslim males could force themselves upon their slaves (in the early period of Islam) or on female prisoners of war. It must be clarified that sexual relations with a female prisoner of war without marrying her, is not at all supported in the Qur'an nor by this specific verse. Reference here is to sexual relationships with those to whom a man is married legally, since sexual relations outside wedlock is totally forbidden. The emphasis or distinction of *malakat aymanuhum* (those whom your right hand possess, meaning [formally] slaves and also prisoners of war) is to indicate that besides marrying amongst the nobility; marry even those who are under your protection (right hand) rather than to indulge in debauchery. This fact is evident from numerous verses in the Qur'an including (4:26) (4:4) (2:222) (24:33). The holy Prophet (pbuh) explicitly states in an authentic tradition, "*A person who has a slave girl and gives her proper education, rears her with dignity, frees her and marries her, for him there is double reward*" (Bukhari).

The only difference between *those whom your right hand possess* and ordinary married woman is that a person cannot marry a married woman, but a prisoner of war or (previously) a slave, could marry the one who is in charge of her; if she so wishes, despite the fact that she may have been married prior to becoming a prisoner. The choice remains hers and there should be no coercion or duress on her.

و الذين هم لاماناتهم و عهدهم راعون

"And those who honor their trusts and fulfill their promises."

Here the truly righteous are referred to as those who take extreme caution in discharging their responsibilities and duties. Elsewhere in the Qur'an, Allah makes reference to the sanctity of fulfilling one's responsibility and maintaining justice when He says, *"Surely, Allah commands you to render back your trusts unto those to whom it is due; and when you judge between people, let it be on the basis of justice."* (Q 4:58)

و الذين هم على صلواتهم يحافظون

"And those who strictly guard their prayer."

There is once again a reference to prayer, but this time it is in the plural (*salawaat*). This could imply the regularity of prayer, the performance thereof in congregation, the performance of supererogatory prayer in addition to the obligatory prayer and the performance of any or all these with sincerity and full consciousness.

Prayer strengthens one's will, reaffirms one's bond with Allah while developing self – discipline and moral rectitude. *"Establish Salaah regularly, for it restrains from evil and corruption."* (Q 29:45)

اولئك هم الوارثون
الذين يرثون الفردوس هم فيها خالدون

"These are the heirs who will inherit Paradise, abiding therein forever."

44

After having mentioned the stages of moral purification and spiritual evolution of the human being, Allah promises the ultimate success to such who are indeed true Believers. The promise here is an eternal reward for a righteous life in this temporary world.

Stages of human creation

ولقد خلقنا الا نسان من سللة من طين

"We have certainly created the human being from a quintessence of clay."

After having made reference to the various stages of the spiritual evolution of a human being the Qur'an now proceeds to describe, in the verses that follow, the various stages of physical development. With this verse begins a description of the process of coming into being of the greatest of Allah's creation – the human being.

Verses like these make reference to natural phenomena and are often referred to as "scientific verses". There are over 750 Qur'anic verses dealing with natural phenomena and though the Qur'an is not to be regarded as a scientific encyclopedia, there are fundamental messages in these verses which command our attention. It must be stated here that the Qur'an is not a textbook of science, nor should any person adapt the Qur'an to changeable scientific theories. These verses are not meant for the teaching of sciences per se, rather they are to be used as an aid to understand the world around us and serve as a means of attracting our attention to the Glory and Majesty of Allah through appreciation of His creation. Modern science makes it easier for us to understand some of these verses, for they contain information not available to people at the time of its revelation.

45

It would be wise for us to ponder over the words of the great former rector of *Al –Azhar* University, *Shaykh Mustafa al – Maraghy* who expressed the following in his introduction to Isma'il Pasha's *Islam and Modern Medicine*: *"It is not my intention to say that this Holy Book contains in detail or in summary all of the sciences in the style of textbooks, rather I want to say that the Qur'an contains general principles by the help of which one can derive all that is needed to know for the physical and spiritual development of human beings. It is infact the duty of the scientists and scholars involved with various sciences to explain for people details that are known to them up to their time ... It is essential for us not to extend the meaning of a Qur'anic verse to such an extent that it enables us to interpret it purely in the light of science, neither should we stretch scientific facts to adapt it to a particular Qur'anic verse. However, if the apparent meaning of a verse is consistent with an established scientific fact, then we interpret the verse with the help of that fact."*

It must be realized that the Qur'an, being Divine, would never be at variance with reality or the facts. There is also no contention between the ideology of Islam and science per se. This is evident even from the writings of early Islamic scholars. Suffice it to quote the great *Imam Abu Hamid al – Ghazali* who wrote: *"All sciences are included in the works and attributes of Allah; while the Qur'an is the explanation of His essence, attributes and works. There are no limits to these sciences and in the Qur'an, there is an indication of their confluence."* (*Ihya 'Ulum al – Deen*)

What we learned from this is that everything that exists is part of Allah's creation and the study of all aspects of nature and the discovery of mysteries of creation is recommended; that everything in this world is orderly and purposeful, operating according to Allah's pattern which is reflected as the law of nature; that all sciences are different manifestations of a world created, decreed and governed by one Supreme Being; and that through appreciation of nature one is bound to reflect upon the Creator.

This verse (Q 23:12) begins to describe the process of human creation from the earliest stage when he/ she lies dormant in the form of dust (*teen*). The inorganic constituent of the earth change through a subtle process and become converted into the life – germ by way of food which human beings ingest. Here we'll find a somewhat detailed reference to the concept of the human embryo being formed in stage from the simple to the more complex. This concept was first scientifically detailed in 1839; over twelve centuries after the demise of the Prophet (pbuh).

The Qur'an evokes our attention by referring to the progressive development of life in the womb and poses the question: "*What is the matter with you that you cannot look towards God's majesty? He has created every one of you in successive stages.*" (Q 71:13 – 14) Allah is indeed the Creator for none can create or bring into existence other than Him. *He is the Creator, the Fashioner and the Bestower of forms* (Q 3:6, 7:11, 40:64, 82:7, 59:24).

Sulalah (mixture and extract of fluids)

The Qur'anic text here makes reference to stages descriptive of external appearance and indicating important developmental events in the process of procreation. Reference to the sperm has been made precisely in (Q 75:37, 86:6, 32:8, 77:20). In Chapter 76 verse 2 the Qur'an states: "*Verily, we have fashioned human beings from a small quantity of mingled*

47

liquids." The term mingled (*amshaj*) could refer to the mixing of the male and female fluids or to the fact that the sperm in itself is formed by various secretions which come from a spermatozoons of the male genital glands, the seminal vesicles, the prostrate gland (which secretes a creamy texture giving the sperm a characteristic odor and color) and the Cooper's gland and Litter's gland giving off mucous.

The word *sulalah* could imply something which is extracted or as the best part of a thing, its quintessence. *sulalah* therefore also indicates a minute extract and is an apt description. As we now know, the sperm constitutes less than one percent of the total semen ejaculated. Nevertheless, ejaculation still contains an average of two hundred and fifty million spermatozoa. It is interesting to note that under normal conditions, only one single cell among these several million will actually penetrate the ovule and therefore an infinitesimally small part of the extract of the sperm is required for procreation to be initiated. This fact was certainly not known at all until the last century. Significantly the holy Prophet (pbuh) referred to this scientific fact when he said, "*Not from the entire fluid which is ejaculated is a human being made, but only from a very small portion of it*" (Muslim). The Qur'anic reference to the scientific fact that only a small volume of liquid produces the necessary effect, is referred to eleven times in the Qur'an.

ثم جعلناه نطفة فى قرار مكين

"*Then We placed it as drop of sperm in a place of rest firmly fixed.*"

<u>*Nutfah* (That which trickles or flows little by little)</u>

The word *nutfah* has been mentioned twelve times in the Holy

48

Qur'an and the Qur'an poses a question, *"Does a human being ever consider out of what substance Allah created him? Out of drops of fluid (nutfah) was he created in which he determined his nature"* (Q 80:17 –19). The fact that we originate from such minute substance and that the genes which determine our characteristics are transferred, is clearly referred to in this verse and is a great source of reflection for us. In another verse Allah states, *"Was he not a mere drop of fluid out of ejaculated semen?... Allah fashioned both male and female from the ejected fluid"* (Q 75:37 – 40). We know that the sex of the newborn is determined by the sperm which will fertilize the ovum. If the sperm carrying X chromosome fertilizes an ovum (which always contain X chromosomes), the offspring will be a girl. If the fertilizing sperm contains a Y chromosome fertilizing the ovum containing the X chromosome then the offspring will be a boy. The above verse makes distinct reference to that scientific fact.

Qararim Makeen (Place of rest firmly fixed)

When the ovum and sperm meets in the fluid medium and fertilization takes place, the sex of the infant to be is genetically determined; the fertilized ovum migrates to the uterus and implantation is completed. The implantation of the egg (ovum) in the uterus (womb) is the result of the development of villosities, (veritable elongation of the egg), which like roots draw nourishment from the thickness of the uterus, necessary for the growth of the ovum. These formations make the egg literally cling to the uterus. The clinging is of course in a place of rest (the womb) and firmly fixed. This act of clinging is described five times in the Qur'an by the word *'alaqah* and as we have made reference to Chapter 75 where Allah says, *"Was the human being not a small quantity of sperm which had emitted? After that he was*

49

something which clings, then Allah fashions him in due proportion."

ثم خلقنا النطفة علقة

"Then We made the drop into a clinging, leech – like structure"

'Alaqah (Clinging and leech – like)

Professor Keith Moore of the University of Toronto Canada, in his work, *A scientist's interpretation of references to Embryology in the Qur'an* states that *the word 'Alaqah refers to a leech or bloodsucker. This is an appropriate description of the human embryo from the seventh to the twenty fourth day when it clings to the endometrium of the uterus, in the same way that a leech clings to the skin. Just as the leech derives blood from the host, the human embryo derives blood from the decidua or pregnant endometrium.*

The term *'Alaqah* presumably describes the outer appearance of the embryo, as well as its relationship with the womb, where the embryo resembles a primitive organism attached to the womb of the host, deriving nutrition by feeding on its blood.

فخلقنا العلقة مضغة

"Then of that leech – like, clinging substance made it into a chewed – like lump"

Mudghah (Chewed – like)

The external appearance of this stage of embryonic development has no particular fixed features except the mark on the edges similar to something which has been bitten on or chewed. This description fits well with the somite stage of embryonic development. The word *Mudghah* is mentioned twice in the Holy Qur'an, once here (Q 23:14) and also in (Q 22:5). However, in Chapter 22, an additional description is given with reference to the fact that certain parts appear to be in proportion while the rest completely out of proportion; (*Mukhallaq,* which signifies shaped in proportion and *Ghayr Mukhallaq,* which implies out of proportion). This is very descriptive of the appearance of the embryo at this stage but also meaningful in the sense that, although there is creation of systems continuing within the womb, the process is incomplete and the matter is like a lump of tissue, irregularly shaped.

فخلقنا المضغة عظاما

فكسونا العظام لحما

"Then We made out of that chewed – like lump bones and clothed the bones with flesh"

Evolving of the skeletal and muscular systems

The Holy Qur'an here states the **mudghah** develops bones and bones are covered by flesh (muscles). Here the somite differentiates into clerotome (from which the skeletal system is formed) and the myotome (from which the muscular system is formed). The Qur'an intimates that bone formation precedes muscles. The Qur'an also makes reference to this at another place where it says, *"Look at the bones how We bring them together and then clothe them with flesh (muscle)"* (Q 2:259). Scientific evidence indicates that the bones form as cartilage models and then the muscles develop around them from the somatic mesoderm.

ثم انشانه خلقا اخر

"Then We cause him to develop into another form"

After the **nutfah** stage [which includes the mixing of the male and female fluids, leading to fertilization, resulting in the embryo forming and taking the appearance of *'alaqah*, developing into the **mudghah** (chewed – like state), followed by the formation of rudimentary cartilage bones being formed and clothed (*kasa*) by muscles (*laham*)]; the embryo develops by the eighth week and takes on a somewhat human appearance with distinctive human features and the initiation of full development of its vital organs. Reference in this part of the verse is to this stage of growth in pre – natal development where the differentiation of parts and organs become manifest and there is a transformation taking place. The human embryo is now called a *fetus* and this may be the "new form" that is being referred to.

Additional facts

Two additional facts are conveyed to us in the Qur'an regarding pre – natal development which are not referred to in Chapter 23, but to which reference is made in Chapters 32 and 39.

1. The description of the appearance of the senses. Allah says *"And He gave you hearing and sight and feeling and understanding"* (Q 32:9). This indicates that a special senses of hearing, seeing and feeling develop in this order. Scientific research indicate that the primordia of the internal ear appear before the beginning of the eyes, and that the brain (the site of understanding giving rise to the faculty of feeling) differentiates last.

In a related matter the holy Prophet (pbuh) said, *"When forty-two days pass after the nutfah settles in the womb it is shaped and receives its hearing, vision, skin, bones and flesh and then it is determined whether it be a boy or a girl"* (Muslim). It is a well – known scientific fact that in the sixth week the zenith of organogenesis (whereby hearing and visual systems, bones, flesh and skin are evolved) is rapidly followed by a differentiation of the gonads into testes or ovaries. Scientific evidence corroborates what the *Hadith* states, for the gonads start to differentiate into testes or ovaries immediately after the hearing and visual systems are settled, and this occurs around the seventh week of intra-uterine life.

2. The Qur'an states; *"Allah makes you in the wombs of your mothers in stages, one after another in three veils of darkness."* (Q 39:6) These <u>three veils</u>, according to modern scientific findings, may refer to the anterior abdominal wall, the uterine wall and the amniochorionic membrane or to the embryo itself which is trilaminar; the outer layer (actoderm), the inner layer (entoderm) and the middle layer (mesoderm).

The actoderm forms the brain, spinal cord, nervous system, sweat glands and the epidermis of the skin with hair. The mouth, lips, palate and some of the canals within the body as well as most parts of the eyes are derived from this actoderm.

The entoderm forms part of the alimentary tract and also the liver, the pancreas and some of the important glands; so too the respiratory tract. The bladder, part of the urethra and part of the genitals are also derived from this entoderm.

The mesoderm forms the entire connective tissue including the cartilages, the bones, the muscles, the kidneys, the blood vessels including much of the genital organs as well as the dermis of the skin.

53

It is significant that Allah mentions these *three veils* or *layers* specifically when making reference to fetal development. This is perhaps due to the fact that the layers or coverings, all play a significant role in the process of facilitating human reproduction. It is important to note that the abdominal wall, the uterine wall and the amniochorionic membrane are each made up of three consecutive layers as well. These serve to protect the fetus from injury by forming a protective cushion, controls the body temperature of the fetus, allows symmetrical growth of the embryo and enables the fetus to move relatively freely, thus aiding development of muscles and bones. Collectively, all the various layers serve the purpose of protection, nutrition, respiration, excretion, hormone production, facilitation of development and growth of the fetus.

Only through Divine information

When we consider the fact that to understand the complex mechanisms of embryonic development, a person first has to possess a thorough knowledge of anatomy, have access to powerful microscopes and be well – grounded in the sciences of physiology, embryology and obstetrics; this knowledge in any of its dimensions was not available even a century ago. So how could an unlettered person living in the middle of the Arabian dessert at the beginning of the seventh century have conveyed these facts with such accurate detail, except through Divine information from the All – Knowing Creator.

The Epigenesis Doctrine (creation of human embryo in successive stages) was first put forward by Dr Wolff in the 18th century and became recognized and accepted late in the nineteenth and early twentieth centuries. In the words of the famous scientific and scriptural scholar, Dr. Maurice Bucaille;

"I consider that the existence in the Qur'an of the verses referring to those concepts (embryology) can have no human explanation on account of the period in which they were formulated." The Canadian scientist and professor of anatomy, Dr Keith Moore says, *"The interpretation of the verse in the Qur'an referring to human development would not have been possible in the 7th century, or even a hundred years ago. We can interpret them now because the science of modern embryology affords us new understandings. Undoubtedly, there are other verses in the Qur'an related to human development that will be understood in the future, as our knowledge increases."*

These signs (*ayaat*) of the Qur'anic verses prove the veracity and truthfulness of the Messenger who conveyed it. After all, it is the duty of the Prophets and Messengers to convey the truth and to bring forth clear signs (4:165) (57:25).

Living in this scientific and technological era, it is most appropriate that the final Messenger (pbuh) should have the Standing Miracle (the Qur'an) reveal scientific facts and incontrovertible truths conveyed through it. As Allah states, *"Surely, herein are signs self – evident in the hearts of those endowed with knowledge, and none but the unjust and those in darkness reject our signs."* (Q 29:49) Furthermore, we had been informed by the Qur'an, that much information will be made manifest to us as time goes by and as human beings develop better modes of understanding the physical world around them. *"Soon, will We show them our signs in the furthest regions of the universe and within themselves* (like fetal development)*, until it becomes manifest to them that this is indeed the Truth. Is it not enough that your Lord is witness unto all things?"* (*Surah Fussilat*: verse 53)

It has been stated unequivocally in the Qur'an that the scientists and scholars are those who are prone to discover some of these Truths. *"And those to whom knowledge has come, see that the revelation sent down to you from your Lord is indeed the Truth; and that it guides to the Path of the Most Exalted, the Praise worthy"* (Q 37:6). In the words of the great contemporary Qur'anic scholar, *'Allama Muhammad Hussein Tabataba'ie; "The Qur'an invites reflection about heavenly signs, the brilliant stars and the differences in their conditions and the systematic order that governs them. The Qur'an encourages meditation concerning the creation of the earth, seas, mountains; the creation of plants, animals, human beings and their inner world. Thus, the Qur'an invites to a study of natural, mathematical and all other fields of science; the learning of which is in the interest of humanity and brings felicity to human society."* (The Qur'an in Islam)

It is the height of academic dishonesty and scientific impropriety to ignore the accurate information and lessons conveyed by these verses of the Holy Qur'an. Allah therefore warns us, *"And those who reject Our sign out of inequity and arrogance despite themselves being convinced of the truth thereof, such should reflect on the end of those who are corrupt and who transgress"* (*Surah An – Naml* verse 14).

فتبارك الله احسن الخالقين
"So blessed be Allah, the Best to Create."

With these words concludes the text which describes in detail the stages of development of the human conceptus. When one comes to have comprehension and realization of the intricacies of embryonic development and the exposition of this information (which was unknown at the time of revelation),

56

one is forced to acknowledge that Allah indeed is the Greatest. Glory to Allah who asks, *"Were human beings created by nothing or were they themselves their own creators? Did they create the heavens and the earth? No, they are on the path of uncertainty"* (Q 52:35 – 36).

As we analyze these verses of the Qur'an, we reflect on the Divine words; *"Surely in the heavens and the earth are signs for those who have Faith. So too, in the creation of yourselves and the animals scattered throughout the worlds; in all these are signs for those assured in Faith"* (Q 46:3 - 4). Indeed, glory to Allah. He is indeed *"the Supreme Being, the Creator, the Evolver and the Bestower of forms. Unto Him belong the most beautiful names and attributes"* (Q 59:24).

ثم انكم بعد ذالك لميتون

"Then you will surely die after a while."

Inevitability of death

After making reference to the spiritual development of the human being and to the development of the human being in the fetal stage before entering this world, the Qur'an now ventures to the inevitable; the end of life in this world through death.

Although the phenomenon of life counts as the most precious of all gifts and though its loss is extremely grievous, none can doubt that just as surely as human being embarks on this life involuntarily to spend some time in this temporary guesthouse which we call the world, each one must ultimately confront the frowning face of death when the scroll of life is rolled up. Whatever comes into existence must traverse a path leading to death (Q 3:185).

Lack of awareness, absence of faith and the failure to adequately comprehend the nature of death, induces dread and insecurity in many human beings, for they make death appear as a terrible nightmare rather than a fact of existence which must come to pass. Specifically those who indulge in evil and those who do not mend their wrongful ways tend to fear death more than others (Q 62:7).

The great poet – philosopher, Moulana Jalal al-Din Rumi said: *"O you who attempt to flee death in fear, it is you yourself that you fear. Use your intelligence! Perhaps it is your countenance that is ugly and not the visage of death, for your soul is a tree on which death is a leaf."* (*Mathnawi*)

ثم انكم يوم القيـمة تبعثون

"Then, on the day of judgment you will be raised up."

Existence beyond the terrestrial

Life is not restricted to this present terrestrial existence which stretches from the moment of birth to the moment of death, for existence is not confined to this physical world. There are basically three states of existence;

The state of effort (*dunya wa 'amal*) which is in this physical world in which a human being can accrue good or evil through his or her deeds.

The second is the intermediate state which is termed *barzukh* and refers to the state between existence on this earth in the physical sense and resurrection in the Hereafter. *Barzukh* literally implies that which is situated between two things. This is the state in which the mortal condition of the human being is dissolved and the soul and body remains separated. The body is buried and the soul without the body is not able to accrue good or evil for it can only do that in relationship with

58

the body.

The third state is that of resurrection (*ba'th*) which everyone will arrive at, for the climax of his or her recompense.

That Creator who is able to bring forth creation by and through His Will, says in the Holy Qur'an; "*Does man not know that We have created him from a mere drop of sperm injected into the womb?* *He then becomes a persistent disputer. He forgets the process of his own creation, but challenges the Supreme Being. He asks how a person shall be revived after his bones has decayed and who has the power to revive him. Tell him, He, Who created creation the first time will indeed be able to revive them.*" (*Surah Ya Sin*, Chapter 36 verses 78 – 80)

SURAH AL – HUJURAAT
CHAPTER 49: VERSES 10 – 13

The principle theme of this *Medinan Surah* is the establishment of concord, amity and goodwill between Muslims. We find mentioned some of the common social evils which cause discord, dissension and bitter differences that corrode, corrupt and contaminate society; thereby destroying the very fiber of the *Ummah*. Since the subject matter of this *surah* is primarily solidarity among members of the Islamic faith; guidelines and directions of conduct calculated to achieve and maintain that solidarity are laid down in the verses under discussion.

We are made to realize that the relationship among members of the *Ummah* is based on consciousness of the universal bond of fraternity which links every Muslim to another; also, the recognition of the sanctity of the rights of others as regards their life, their property and their honor. It is prohibited in Islam to contravene or threaten the above in word or deed while the degree of prohibition is directly proportionate to the magnitude of the material or moral harm which could result from it.

انما المؤمنون اخوة

فاصلحوا بين اخويكم واتقوا الله لعلكم ترحمون

"Surely, the Believers are one fraternity, so make peace and reconciliation between your bretheren; be sincerely dutiful and conscious of Allah in order that you may receive His mercy."

Ukhuwwah (fraternity of Believers)

In this ayah there is mention of _ukhuwwah_ (brotherhood),
islaah (reconciliation), _taqwa_ (dutiful God – consciousness)
and _rahmah_ (Divine mercy). As regards the brotherhood of
Believers, they are united through the bond of faith. The holy
Prophet emphasized the necessity for developing the spirit of
Islamic brotherhood in practical terms by insisting that it be
expressed tangibly in the form of mutual help and concern.

The brotherhood mentioned is of course not one of genealogy
but one which is in fact stronger than the bond of blood; it is
the bond of faith. The Holy Prophet (pbuh) said in this regard;
_"The Believers are like one structure each part supporting the
other"_ (Muslim). To encourage the engendering of love and
affection amongst the community of faith and to confirm that
this brotherhood was not just theoretical but evident in actual
practice, the holy Prophet remarked: _"None of you truly
believes until he loves for his brother what he loves for
himself"_ (Bukhari). Furthermore, in a hadith (documented by
Imam Muslim) the greatest guide to humanity (pbuh) is
reported to have said: _"Allah is at the aide of a servant as long
as the servant helps his brother."_ It is also evident from
numerous verses of the Qur'an and traditions of the holy
Prophet that we should become _"brothers in the service of
Allah."_

Islaah (Maintaining good relationships and reconciling one which is in tatters)

Since the Muslim society is based on mutual care and co –
operation, the stress on brotherhood is part of the strength of
the Muslim community. The power of Islam in action lies in
the ideal of the Fraternity of the _Ummah_, which transcends the
barriers of cast, color, gender, geographical boundary or

economic status. We are therefore advised in the Holy Qur'an (Ch 8:46) to avoid unnecessary disputes which cause division, weakness and dissipation of power. It is in this spirit that Muslims are forbidden to keep apart from his fellow Muslim for more than three days. It is most important to maintain cordial relationships and more specifically the maintenance of relations with blood relatives. The holy Prophet has admonished the Believers in the following words, " *One who cuts of relationships unduly will not enter Paradise*" (Bukhari). Estrangement and enmity are not part of the makeup of the relationship of a Muslim towards another and therefore the Qur'an highlights the significance of the bond between Believers in this verse by saying: "***Surely the Believers are a fraternity. Make reconciliation between members of this fraternity.***"

In order to draw our attention to the dangers of conflict and hostility amongst Believers, the holy Prophet said: "*Shall I inform you of something higher in value than fasting, charity and prayer?*" *on receiving an affirmative reply he said: "It is to make reconciliation between brothers, for to incite people to dispute is like a razor, it does not shave of the hair but shreds the religion*" (Tibrani).

We are reminded about the Fraternity of Believers (*ukhuwwah*) and the need for reconciliation (*islaah*) between this universal community; all this, with (*taqwa*) sincere, dutiful obedience and consciousness of Allah that we may be blessed by His (*rahmah*) infinite Mercy.

يـاايهـا الـذيـن امـنـوا لا يـسـخـر قـوم مـن قـوم عـسـى
ان يـكـونـوا خيرا مـنـهم ولا نـسـاء
مـن نـسـاء عـسـى ان يـكـن خـيـرا مـنـهن
ولا تـلـمـزوا انـفـسـكم ولا تـنـابـزوا بالالقا ب
بـئـس الاسـم الفـسـوق بـعد الايمـان
و مـن لـم يـتـب فـاولئـك هم الظـلـمـون

"O Believers, let not some men among you scorn or mock
at others, perhaps the latter may be better than the
former. Neither should women scorn and mock other
women, perhaps the latter may be better than the former.
Neither discredit each other nor abuse each other with
offensive nick–names. The worst of names or titles is that
of immorality or impropriety after faith; and whosoever
does not repent are truly of the wrongdoers."

In order to realize and maintain the spirit of true brotherhood,
Allah has prescribed a number of directives related to the
preservation of that brotherhood and therefore has laid down
certain prohibitions which must be abided by in order to
practically establish the brotherhood referred to in the
previous verse.

Undermining the worth of others as human beings (*Sukhriyyah*).

The first prohibition is *Sukhriyyah*, which implies mocking,
scoffing, deriding or denigrating another. These are generally
a by-product of arrogance and pride where one considers
himself or herself superior to another while considering the

other to be inferior. If we as Muslims were to analyze history we would find the first sin (original sin, if you wish) to have occurred when *Iblis* refused to acknowledge the station of Adam; due to the arrogance of *Iblis*; despite the command of God. When people undermine others it is normally due to race, physical features; social, economic or political status. All this is not recognized in the Supreme Court of Allah, as the holy Prophet (pbuh) said: *"Allah does not judge you by your physical features nor your wealth, but He evaluates you by the sincerity of your hearts and the deeds which emanate from it"* (Musilm). In the history of Islam we find *Bilal*, the beloved companion of the holy Prophet (and the first *Muathin* of Islam) closer to the Prophet as his companions and dearer to the *Ummah*, though he was formally an Abassinian slave; yet, Abu Lahab, who was the most noble of the nobility of the *Quraish* and an uncle of the Prophet, is far removed from the Prophet and from the *Ummah*. This reinforces the concept of the bond of brotherhood through faith being higher in value than the bond of blood outside faith.

We must acknowledge, *"all human beings are descendents of Adam and Adam was created from the lowest of matter"* (Abu Dawood). It is little wonder that the Prophet severely warned against harboring any feeling of superiority or pride by saying: *"Anyone who has the extent of an atom's weight of pride in his heart will not enter Paradise."* (Tirmidhi)

Character assassination and verbal abuse (*Lamz and Nabaz*)

The next step in establishing the brotherhood and maintaining ideal relationship involves the duel prohibition against the habit of discrediting and name calling. Slander or character assassination and the habit of publicly exposing the faults and shortcomings of others are totally prohibited. The holy Prophet is reported to have said: "*Whososever covers the faults of a Muslim, Allah will cover his faults on the Day of Resurrection*" (Tirmidhi).

The word *lamz* literally means piercing or stabbing and is indicative of those who undermine others through faultfinding. Since the Qur'an considers the community of Believers as one brotherhood regarding its mutual concerns and responsibilities, thus it considers slandering of a fellow Muslim as in fact slandering the self.

As regards *nabaz*, it needs to be stated that pet names which are not offensive in meaning nor disliked by the person is acceptable. This is clearly evident from the Prophet referring to Sayyidina 'Ali as "*Abu Turaab*" (*father of dust*), because on an occasion 'Ali was lying on the ground covered with dust; or perhaps reference to 'Ali's caring for the poor (the down trodden laying in the dust). What is forbidden is to abuse a person by titles of immorality or of mockery. No form of verbal abuse; whether by slandering or by offensive names, should be indulged in. It is in this regard that the holy Prophet is reported to have said that: "*A Muslim is that person from whose hands and tongue other Muslims are safe.*"

The verse goes on to suggest that if anyone has been guilty of mocking, slandering or being verbally offensive in any way, to repent or else they would be of the wrongdoers. As regards the concept of repentance (*taubah*), four basic conditions have to be fulfilled. These conditions are essential in confirming the sincerity of the repentant and indicative of his genuineness:
To be truly sorry and to regret (*nadam*);
To make *Taubah* in the literal sense, meaning *to turn away*

(*taaba*) from the wrongful act;
Not to repeat the act;
To effect restitution by trying to rectify the situation and return the status quo as far as possible.

يا ايها الذين امنوا اجتنبوا كثيرا من الظن
ان بعض الظن اثم ولا تجسسوا ولا يغتب بعضكم
بعضا ايحب احدكم ان ياكل لحم اخيه ميتا
فكرهتموه واتقوا الله ان الله تواب رحيم

"O Believers, avoid much suspicion for surely some suspicion is sinful. Neither spy on each other nor backbite one another. Would any of you like to eat the flesh of his dead brother? Certainly you would detest it. So be sincerely dutiful to Allah; for verily, Allah is oft - forgiving, Most Merciful."

Elimination of suspicion (*Zann*)

Having prohibited, in clear terms, the outer negative factors like character assassination and verbal abuse; the Qur'an turns to the inner or more secretive forms of negative behavior. The outer expression of brotherhood cannot truly exists and operate without the inner qualities of trust, mutual confidence fellow feeling. Be rest assured that the Islamic system aims at establishing a society based on mutual trust and clearness of conscience. In that scheme; suspicions, doubts, mistrusts and accusations are to be eliminated. In a Prophetic statement documented in Bukhari, the holy Prophet advised: *"Beware of expressing suspicion, for verily that is the most deceptive form of speech"* (Muslim). We are encouraged to think the best and speak the best of our fellow Muslims and as Caliph 'Umar is reported to have said, *"If a fellow Muslim makes an ambiguous statement, think the best of it and you'll find a good explanation therefor"* (Muwatta).

Invasion of privacy (*Tajassus*)

Inward mistrust, suspicion and uncontrolled curiosity produces evil thoughts while outwardly it leads a person towards the despised practice of unnecessarily concerning one's self with the private affairs of others. Since the Islamic way of life is meant to establish a society on inner and outer purity, we find the prohibition of spying following immediately that of suspicion. The holy Prophet recommended; *"Among the things which completes a person's Islam is his avoidance of those things which do not concern him"* (Tirmidhi). He further classified those who seek out people's shortcomings as being hypocrites. Abdullah ibne 'Umar narrates that the holy Prophet mounted the pulpit and called out in a loud voice: *"O you who declare Islam with your tongues but who's hearts have not been reached by faith, do not annoy the Muslims nor seek out their faults, for the one who seeks out the faults of his fellow Muslim will have his faults exposed by Allah"* (Ibn Majah).

Numerous other traditions of the Prophet indicate the strong abhorrence of spying and invading the privacy of others. *"Blessed is he who is more concerned with his own shortcomings than concerning himself with the faults of other"* (Al – Bazaar*). "The habitual eavesdropper will not enter Paradise"* (Tibrani). Spying is discredited to such and extent that Islamic Law rejects evidence obtained through spying. The Qur'an highly regards the right of privacy (Qur'an 24:27 – 28) and the Prophet is further reported to have said: *"If* *you seek out the faults of people, you may corrupt them or bring them close to corruption"* (Ibn Habban).

Destruction of integrity (consumption of human flesh) (*Gheebah*)

The evil of *gheebah* is nothing but desire to deride the integrity of others in their absence. It is certainly an expression of hypocrisy and cowardice. In order to bring to our attention the vileness of this destructive habit, the Qur'an paints a repulsive picture of *gheebah* by equating it to *the eating of dead human flesh.* The holy Prophet (pbuh) defined *gheebah* in such clear terms as leaves absolutely no room for misunderstanding; *"Gheebah is mentioning something about another which he dislikes." When he was asked what if what was said were true? The Prophet (pbuh) replied: "If what you said about him in his absence was true you have back bitten him; and if it was not true you have slandered him"* (Muwatta). This evil of backbiting have become so common in modern day society that most people do not realize the evil they are indulging in. Imam al – Shaf'ie beautifully captured this in one of his poems: *"Never do you find the flesh – eating wolf eating the flesh of another wolf, but how often do we eat the flesh of one another."*

To encourage the opposite of *gheebah* and to reduce the possibility of our indulgence in this filthy habit, the Prophet (pbuh) said: *"If any person defends another who is slandered in his absence, it will be his due from Allah to set him free from the fire of hell"* (Musnad Ahmad). The holy Prophet (pbuh) furthermore encouraged us in this regard by saying: *"On the Day of Resurrection, Allah will protect from the fire the one who defended the honor and integrity of his fellow Believer in his absence"* (Tirmidhi).

A despicable habit which is usually associated with slander, suspicion and backbiting and one which is equally prohibited in Islam is that of gossiping. Gossiping (*namimah*) implies conveying to others what you hear from someone else in manner which causes dissension among people, creates rivalry and bad feeling, or increases existing feuds or bitterness between people. The habit of the gossippers has been well captured in the words of an Arab poet who said; *"If the gossippers hear a good word about someone they hide it, if they hear a bad word they shout it, and if they hear nothing they create lies and spread it."* The Qur'an refers to those who indulge in this diabolical practice as despicable and slanderous (Q 68:10 – 11), (Q 49:6), (Q 104:1 – 5). The holy Prophet (pbuh) is reported to have said: " *The one who spreads gossip which he has overheard will not enter Paradise"* (Bukhari). It is thus a distinct fact that the Islamic teachings safeguard human honor, human integrity and human dignity; regarding them as inviolable and sacred. Abdullah ibn 'Umar, a well known companion of the Prophet Muhammad (pbuh), on an occasion looked at the Ka'bah and remarked; *"How great and sacred you are! Yet, the sanctity of the Believer is greater than yours."*

Many of the evils that have been mentioned in these two verses have been referred to in a well – known tradition in which the holy Prophet (pbuh) is reported to have said: *"I warn you concerning suspicion because the expression of suspicion could be the worst of lies. Do not undermine one another, neither spy on one another, nor be envious of one another, nor harbor dislike for one another, neither denigrate nor disappoint one another (by treachery); but rather be servants of Allah as one brotherhood"* (Muslim).

The underlying theme of these verses is the promotion of

husn-ul-khuluq (good moral character and righteous conduct). There is a tradition, transmitted on the authority of Anas ibn Malik who said: "*Someone asked: 'O Messenger of Allah, which of the Believers is the most excellent in faith?' To this he replied; 'The best of them in moral character (ahsanu – hum khuluqan).*"

The great saintly personality, Sheikh Abdul Qadir Jilani (Allah's Mercy be upon him) said; "*Good moral character (khulqun hasan) is the most excellent of all the virtues of the servant (of the Lord), and through it the essential natures (jawahir) of men are made manifest. The human being is privately disguised by his physical constitution (khalq), and publicly revealed by his moral character (khuluq).*
Allah (Almighty and Glorious is He) has distinguished His Prophet and His Messenger, Muhammad (Allah bless him and give him peace), by endowing him with certain miracles (mu'jizat), charismatic exploits (karamat), and exceptional virtues (fada'il). Yet, He has not praised him for any of his special qualities, to the same extent as He has praised him for his moral character (khuluq), for He has said (More Glorious is He than any other sayer); 'And you are indeed of a splendid character.' (68:4)
Several explanations have been offered, including the following; "When Allah extolled him on account of his moral character (khuluq), He did so because he behaved with noble generosity in both the material and the spiritual realms of being and because he was completely satisfied with Allah."
(*Al – Ghunya Li Talibi Tariq Al – Haq*)

70

Magna Carta of human fraternity

يا ايها الناس انا خلقناكم من ذكر و انثى
وجعلناكم شعوبا وقبائل لتعارفوا
ان اكرمكم عند الله اتقكم
ان الله عليم خبير

"O human kind! We have surely created you from male and female and made you into peoples and organized communities in order that you may know and recognize each other. Certainly, the most noble and honorable of you (in the estimation of Allah) are those who are most sincerely dutiful and God-conscious. Surely, Allah is All-knowing, Most Informed."

In this verse the Divine address shifts from the specific to the general, from the Believers to all human beings; moving from the discussion of the brotherhood of Believers to the universal human family. Here the false notions of racial arrogance, chauvinism, conceit, sexism and arrogance that emanates from tribalism, racism, nationalism and economic advantage are put to the axe. By mentioning the origin of all human beings as emanating from male and female (Adam and Eve) we are reminded of our common ancestry. Emphasis is also laid on the complimentary roles of male and female in relation to human society.

The grandeur and greatness of Allah is reflected in his creativity which is manifested in bringing forth creation, reflecting an infinite diversity, yet originating from a unity.

71

Reference to the diversity of people as reflected through the societies, communities, nations and tribes; some of which are based on family ties which define the boundaries of marriage, incest; delineating family obligations, rights and duties of people.

The Standard of human excellence (*Taqwa*)

The only real and true criterion of human greatness in the estimation of the Divine is *Taqwa* (sincere, dutiful consciousness of Allah). The holy Prophet (pbuh) conveyed the significant criterion of human excellence, in his own inimitable way, on the occasion of the farewell pilgrimage at Makkah, shortly before breathing his last; *"O people! Your God is one and your ancestor is one; there's no superiority of any Arab over any nor Arab, nor of a non Arab over any Arab. There is no superiority of a white over the red nor of the red over the white, but only to the extent to which each individual discharges his duty to Creator and creation. The most honored among human beings in the sight of Allah are those who are most righteous."* (Baihaqi)

In these verses we are reminded of the supra – national bond between Believers as people of Faith and social evils, which if not effectively checked, could erode the vitals of a society and undermine its whole social structure. The social evils which are most pronounced and far reaching in its evil consequences are mocking, verbal abuse, suspicion, spying, backbiting, conceit, false pride, chauvinism and racialism. As part of the greater human family we are reminded by the God of all creation that the standard of human excellence is piety; a quality that emanates from internal purity of intention that manifests itself through righteous conduct.

BASIS FOR THE IDEAL SOCIAL ORDER

(CHAPTER 2:V 177)

Practical expression of welfare is the fabric of faith

The pattern of universal goodwill and welfare is interwoven in every fabric of Islamic doctrine, legislation and practice. With such gravity does Islam view this obligation (of universal welfare) that none can righteously claim inclination to the Divine Universal Way of Life (Islam) without first furnishing practical proof of selfless commitment to this humanitarian ideal...

In the words of the Prophet (pbuh); "*None of you have Faith unless he prefers for others what he prefers for himself.*
None of you can righteously claim to Believe until and unless you sacrifice for others that which you yourself love most.
The highest expression of Faith is... that you love for humanity that which you love for yourself and despise for humanity that which you dislike for yourself."

Thus the customary flimsy claim to belief by mere pronouncing of certain formulae or the mere performance of certain rituals does not *per se* make one a true Believer. Belief is coupled with true commitment to the Divine in every sphere of activity.

ليس البر ان تولوا وجوهكم قبل المشرق و المغرب
و لكن البر من امن بالله و اليوم الاخر

و الملائكة و الكتاب و النبيين
و اتى المال على حبه ذوى القربى
و اليتامى و المساكين و ابن السبيل
و السائلين و فى الرقاب
و اقام الصلوة و اتى الزكوة
و الموفون بعهدهم اذا عاهدو
و الصابرين فى البأساء و الضراء و حين الباس
اولئك الذين صدقوا
و اولئك هم المتقون

It is not righteousness that you turn
Your faces towards East or West;
But it is righteousness – To
Believe in Allah and the Last Day,
and the Angels, and the Book,
and the Messengers; to spend of
your substance, out of love for
Him, For your kin, for orphans,
for the needy, for the wayfarer,
for those who ask, and for the
ransom of those in bondage; to be steadfast
in prayer, and practice regular
charity; to fulfil the contracts
which you have made; and to be
firm and patient, in pain,
suffering, adversity and
throughout all periods of panic.
Such are the People of Truth, the
Allah – conscious. (2:177)

Fundamental principles of the Ideal Social Order

It is not righteousness to ritually turn your face towards East or West; But righteousness is that you believe...
In Allah:
The Supreme Authority, the Uncaused First Cause who is the Eternal Source and Origin of all existence and in Whom is inherent all manifestations of perfection.

And the Last Day:
A future time period of accountability where each individual will be held responsible and accountable for his or her worldly deeds.

And the Angels:
Who are the Divine functionaries of Allah.

And the Book:
Though we accept all Divine scriptures like the Original Bible, Original Taurah, ... unfortunately (due to interpolation and alterations) none of the scriptures have been preserved in their original pristine form, except the Holy Qur'an, *the Book*.

And all the Prophets:
Islam is the only Faith that has it as an article of faith to believe in all the Prophets that were sent to all the various peoples throughout history. In essence, they all brought the same message to different people at different periods. Their message was based on Divine Covenant aimed at establishing the universal, natural, true Way of Life; leading to the implementation of the social system of Goodness and Justice. *"We sent our Prophets with clear Guidance and Scriptures, containing the ideal Criterion (and Balance) for the express purpose that humanity may establish justice."* (Q 57:25)

And out of the love for Allah, to avail what you possess for the benefit of those dear to you, the orphans, the needy, the wayfarers, those who ask, and for the freeing of those in bondage:

After proclaiming inclination to Islam one is required to give practical expression to this inclination by offering whatever abilities, flair, art, comfort, wealth, possession... that one has been entrusted with, for the benefit of humanity. It is with reference to this that the holy Prophet (pbuh) said: *"Most certainly, Deen is expressed in man's treatment of fellow human beings."*

Whatever we possess belongs to Allah; we are only trustees thereof. Whatever we are graced with in this world (whether it be knowledge, wealth, political power...) we are entrusted with these as vicegerents of Allah and we are to be accountable for each aspect of our trusteeship. Such is our responsibility towards the needy, downtrodden and oppressed that the Almighty Himself proclaims: *"And why should you not fight in the cause of Allah and the oppressed men, women and children, whose cry is – O our Lord! Save us from this place whose people are oppressors. Raise us from Thee one who will help us, one who will assist us."* (Q 4:75)

The true Muslim, committed to the universal welfare presented by Islam, is the one who is duty – bound to rise in assistance of these oppressed, for the true Believer is part of that ideal Global Community (the *Ummah*) which has been evolved for the benefit of humanity (Q 3:110).

And establish regular Prayer (Salaah):

Prayer is the *spiritual elevation of the Believer* due to the fact that during *Salaah* the worshipper devotes his entire attention to his Creator without any intermediate, materialistic interference. The objective to be achieved is documented in the Holy Qur'an, *"Establish prayer, for most certainly prayer*

76

prevents from shameful deeds, indecency, all forms of evil, corruption, exploitation; and the constant awareness of Allah is the greatest of virtues." (Q 29:45)

The concept of prayer is not mere ritual devoid of Divine commitment and social welfare for the holy Prophet (pbuh) intimated that *there are those who pray yet achieve nothing by their prayer except tiredness from bowing and prostration. Allah only accepts the prayer of those who are humble and sincere, those who do not exceed the limits, those who meet the needs of the needy and who feed the hungry.*

Thus the establishing of *Salaah* is akin to the pursuance of spiritual and moral welfare.

And establish Zakaah (prescribed charity):

Islam does not presuppose a class system of 'haves' giving meager handouts to the 'have-nots'. In Islam, everything belongs to Allah. Man is only the trustee of what he possesses and *whatever is in his possession beyond his basic needs is to be availed to those who need it.* The holy Prophet (pbuh) said: *"In the possession of those who have lies the right of those who do not have."*

So after having provided welfare assistance to the best of your ability, if anything is left in your possession in excess of your basic needs, then *Zakaah* is still the prescribed obligatory tax on that. The establishing of *Zakaah* therefore is akin to the pursuance of economic welfare.

To fulfill obligations and promises you have made:

Indeed Islam is the order wherein it is obligatory to be true in thought, word and deed. Fulfillment of duty, responsibility and commitments is part of that obligation.

And to patiently persevere throughout all periods of panic and hardship:

All the above conditions have to be included and practically

77

fulfilled for one to be a true Believer.

These are those who are truthful, they are the sincerely committed.

The requirements that have been laid down in this single verse of the Holy Qur'an (Chapter 2:Verse 177) contain the basic elements for that *Ideal Social Order* propagated by Islam... the Social Order of Truth, Justice and Goodness.

SURAH AL-MA'UN
Acts of Kindness / Service to the Needy
(Chapter 107)

This *surah* is a Makkan revelation according to the majority of Quranic scholars. According to some authorities this is a Makkan-Madinan revelation (The first three verses are said to have been revealed in Makkah and the rest in Madinah). Yet this *surah* in its theme and structure is one interwoven entity, aiming at the establishment of one of the most fundamental aspects of faith. It must be added here that the strongest evidence favors the view that the whole *surah* was revealed early in the Makkan period.

The *surah* deals with two basic principles of Islam whose neglect constitutes denial of religion itself and could be construed as disregard for the consequences of accountability on the Day of Judgement. These principles are: worship of Allah and service to humanity.

The title of this *surah* is taken from the word "*al-ma'un*" with which the *surah* ends.

ارءيت الذي يكذب بالدين
"Have you observed the person who belies the Faith and denies the Judgement."

This *surah* starts with a perplexing question addressed to all those who can use the faculty of thought and perception, generating suspense and holding their attention in order to make them reflect and realize the aim, the subject and the moral of this *surah*. Have you observed, or reflected on *the person who falsifies, misrepresents the Deen of Islam*, or *who undermines the final authority and comprehensiveness of the Final Judgement?*

It must be noted here that the word **al-Deen** is the infinitive noun from Arabic which means "he obeyed / earned." The word "*Deen*", by implication, could be construed to mean: requital, recompense, judgement or reckoning, predominance or ascendancy, mastery or rule, religious organization, righteousness, state or condition, Divine decree, habit, custom; or religion in general.

In view of the different meanings of *Deen*, this first verse may signify reference to the person who has no faith in Divine Reckoning; or one who disobeys and defies propriety to the community or society or ideological grouping to which he belongs; or one who does not believe that religion is the ultimate source of morals; or one with whom the doing of good does not become a habit; or one who does not conform his conduct to Divine Decree and thus does not develop in himself divine attributes; or one who does not worship Allah with true and sincere devotion. We can thus deduce that the word "*Deen*" includes in its signification all those things which are moral, beneficial and done with commitment, consciousness and sincerity.

فذالك الذي يدع اليتيم
ولا يحض علي طعا م المسكين

"That is the person who repulses the orphan without care or consideration and does not concern himself nor encourages others to feed the poor and help the needy"

The word *yadu'ue*, though implying harsh or rough action, could include misappropriation, usurpation, repulsing, insulting, disgracing and denigrading any orphan. The Holy Qur'an has not only urged us to give the orphans their rights but also reprimands those who do not give them respect. (*Surah* 89, verse 17)

In the preceding verse we were told that denial of religion or of the Final Reckoning opens the way to heedlessness and a sense of non-accountability. These verses speak of perhaps the two most deadly ills of society, which if not scrupulous guarded against, could bring about the decline and disintegration of a community;
The failure to take proper care of the orphans (this kills in people the spirit of sacrifice, of sharing and caring).
Neglect of the poor and needy (which deprives a useful section of the society the initiative and the will to improve their condition).
These verses represent one of the two basic principles of Islam, *huquq al'ibad* (service to humanity). The Holy Prophet in numerous *ahadith* made reference to this spirit of service and goodwill to humanity as "*shafaqatu'ala khalqillah*".

The verbs used in both these *ayats* **yadu'ue** and **yahuddu** are used in the future tense and thus the case indicate the continuity of such actions in regard to orphans and the poor. It must be noted that to feed the needy is in itself a virtuous deed, irrespective of whether the needy person be a Muslim or a non-Muslim; and to be harsh to an orphan is a sinful act in all conditions whatever religion, ideology or community the orphan may belong to. We also realize from these *ayaat* that if we cannot feed the hungry by ourselves then we must encourage others who are able to, to do so. What is most significant to note is that at the time when this *surah* was revealed the number of Muslims in Makkah was very small and the Muslim community was still in its infancy, yet the command to feed the poor and help the needy at the inception of Islamic society is proof that Islam wants to create in its followers that feeling of human sympathy, whose sphere of influence is vast enough to cover the entire humanity and on the basis of which every deserving person should be helped.

As regards the response to the question about the one who *denies the Judgement* or the *Deen* of Islam, these two verses give a direct response. *It is the one who harshly repels the orphan and does not care nor urges others to feed the poor.* This definition of disbelief or false claimant to belief may surprise some when compared with the traditional understanding and definition of faith, but this is the root of the whole issue. Indeed the one who misrepresents the faith is the person who is wicked, harsh, humiliating, careless and selfish. If the truth of Islam had in any way affected his heart, such a person would never treat the most needy members of society (and creation of Allah) with such harshness and would neither manifest a non-chalant attitude of this nature. True belief then, is not mere utterance of the mouth, but an overall change of the individual's heart and attitude, motivating him to benevolence and goodwill for all human beings, especially those that are in need of his care, attention or assistance.

فويل للمصلين الذين هم عن صلاتهم ساهون
"Shame unto those worshippers who are unmindful (concerning the dimensions of) their prayer"

The unconscious worshippers have been singled out here as unmindful of the nature and the true purpose of prayer since their prayer fails to bring about in them a moral change which prayers are intended to create and the social consciousness that the *jama'ah* ought to develop in the worshipping person.

82

Prayer represents the duties and obligations we owe to Allah and they are called *huquq – Allah* (obligations due to Allah – the first basic principle of Islam). These verses also purport that the prayers of those hypocritical persons who do not discharge the obligations they owe to Allah's creations (*huquq al-'ibad*, obligations due to humanity at large) are like a body without a soul, a shell without substance. Their actions tend to be superficial and hypocritical, which instead of doing them good adds to their hypocrisy. They are those who put on a show of piety, who execute the mechanical aspects and pronounce the verbal formulae of prayer, but their hearts are not receptive to them, neither are they enriched by praying, nor is their social consciousness awakened. Thus the essence and purpose of prayer and its components are not present in their psyche. They offer prayer merely as exercise or a habit; perhaps to impress or deceive others, but not out of true devotion to Allah and His commands regarding himself and the rest of creation. Muslims, it must be remembered, are obliged to offer their prayer regularly, bearing in mind that these prayers are a manifestation of their servitude to Allah in all aspects of life and indicates commitment to the comprehensive commands of the Creator.

The term *sahun* is derived from *sahu* which implies a *mistake done unintentionally* or *a wrong done neglectfully*. In the first case one could be excused, but in the second case one is not. Here, *sahun* purports negligence with guilt. So being unmindful of prayer could be construed as meaning not paying heed to the spirit of prayer, and prayer in *jama'ah* specifically should motivate members of the *jama'ah* to care for the *jama'ah* as they care for themselves.

83

الذين هم يرا ءون ويمنعون الما عون

*"Those who perform ostentatious prayer (prayer for show)
yet refuse and refrain from helping others"*

Prayer for show is bereft of sincerity and is merely a prayer of soulless display and hypocrisy which is done in order that people may think of the worshipper as being pious and religious. Such display their prayfulness and their would-be piety to the public. Once again, we find the Holy Qur'an presents the fundamental nature and spirit of prayer. Any semblance of servitude which is intended for show and not devoted to Allah; that kind of prayer that has not affected their hearts, their behavior and thus not motivated them to selfless service for the benefit of those they are able to assist; to such hypocrites Allah says; *"fa waylul lilmusallin"* (woe to such worshippers).

In connection with such hypocrisy there are statements of Nabi 'Isa (Jesus, Peace be Upon Him) which are quoted in the Book of Matthew verse 6, where he is reported to have said *"Beware of practicing your piety before people in order to be seen by them. When you give alms sound no trumpet before you as the hypocrites do in the places of worship and in the streets, so that they may be praised by the people. Truly I say to you they have already received their rewards (the accolades of the people for whom they are showing off). But when you give charity, do not let your left hand know what your right hand is doing; and when you pray you must not be like hypocrites for they love to stand and pray in places of worship and in public so that people may see them."*

Further on in Matthew, Nabi 'Isa (Peace be Upon Him) said: *"Shame on you, scribes and Pharisees, hypocrites! Who*

84

devour widows' houses and for pretense you make long prayers wherefore you will receive great condemnation. Shame on you, scribes and Pharisees, hypocrites! For you clean the outside of the cup but inside you are full of filth. Shame on you scribes and Pharisees, hypocrites! You are like a white – washed tomb, which outwardly appears beautiful, but within they are full of dead man's bones and all uncleanliness. So you also outwardly appear righteous to people but inside you are full of hypocrisy and injustice." (Matthew, verse 23)

It would be appropriate here to reflect upon the famous *hadith* of the holy Prophet Muhammad (pbuh) *"Actions will be judged and evaluated according to the intention that motivates the action. And each person will be rewarded according to his or her intention."*

The *surah* concludes with the word *al – ma'un* which is also the title of the surah. *Al – ma'un* refers to the necessities of life, articles of common use; can refer to *zakah*, acts of kindness, good deeds or helping others in general. In its wider sense it denotes *aid* and *assistance* in any difficulty. *Al – ma'un* is explained by Imam Bukhari (R.A.) as meaning *al – ma'ruf kulluhu* (that is *every good*, or *kind* or *charitable deed*). And Ikrama (according to Bukhari), considers the highest form of *ma'un* to be *zakah* and the lowest form to be *assisting others with basic useful things*; thus, according to Bukhari, *al – ma'un* includes *all acts of kindness or assistance offered to fellow human beings*.

In the last two verses of this *surah*, two major issues are brought to our attention:
One is hypocrisy, where prayer is done for show and not performed sincerely;

Secondly, refusal to supply basic assistance to the needy. This indicates that whatever is for Allah the insincere ones do and perform to show people, and whatever is for the benefit of people they refuse to fulfill. Here we call to mind the words of our master Muhammad (pbuh) who is reported to have said: *"Allah is at the assistance of a person as long as that person is of assistance to his fellow human beings."*

Serve the Creator and creation

This chapter gives expression to the prominence, which Islam gives to helping the needy and uplifting the poor. Anyone who pays no attention to this is spoken of as one who has *belied the Religion* and *undermined the Judgement.* Prayer to Allah and help to the poor are repeatedly spoken of in the Holy Qur'an as foundations of Islam. But we are told, in this *surah*, that even prayer is mere show and hollow if it does not generate feelings of love, sympathy and fellow – feeling. Islam is not a way of life built on ostentation and superficiality. Different aspects of Islamic acts of worship are meaningless if they are purely mechanical, unless motivated by sincerity, commitment and devotion. Sincere worship produces effects within the individual's heart, which should cause him to act righteously, fairly, justly and in a balanced way. This will be reflected in his social behavior.

The essence of Faith, if firmly rooted in the hearts and minds of people, must immediately operate behaviorally through the person and manifest itself in the person's attitude, expression and actions. The *surah* stresses that if that is not the case, then where is the faith, truly speaking. The qualities of despising orphans, refusing to feed the hungry or assist the needy, being heedless of the prescribed prayer, showing off, hypocrisy and not being co – operative with the people; illustrates

86

miserliness, conceit and such persons have neither connection with the people nor true association with the Creator. The holy Prophet (pbuh) is reported to have said: *"Surely the selfish person is far from Allah, far from people, far from the Jannah, close to the Fire; but the charitable, helpful person is close to Allah, loved by people, close to the Jannah and far from the Fire."*

From this thought-provoking *surah*, we gather the intent behind what Allah demands of us when He instructs us to believe in and worship Him. Allah is free of all wants and thus seeks no benefit for Himself, but He cares for the welfare and prosperity, the purification and happiness of His creation. The Creator wishes human life to be elevated, happy, based on pure motives and characterized by mutual compassion, brotherhood, purity of heart, clear conscience, unwavering commitment and beneficial behavior.

SURAH AL – TAKAATHUR (MATERIAL CONTENTION) CHAPTER 102

Surah Al – Takaathur takes its name from the first verse. According to all commentators, this *surah* is by all accounts a Makkan revelation in view of its contents and style. The *surah* basically deals with the very common yet deadly social and spiritual disease of vying with one another in the accumulation and amassing of material things; taking pride in their abundance, while forgetting the temporary nature of life and the impermanence of material things.

The holy Prophet (pbuh) was greatly concerned about the possibility of his followers indulging in this destructive mutual rivalry for worldly gains that he is reported to have said; *"By Allah, I am not afraid that you will become poor, but I am afraid that you will acquire worldly wealth in abundance as it was given to peoples before you, and you will start competing with each other as they did, and it would divert you as it diverted them"* (Bukhari).

الهاكم التكا ثر

"*Accumulation diverts you*"

The word *Takaathur* implies contending with one another for things of the world which often become a source of arrogance, a feeble (and false) source of superiority. Acquisition of wealth and the human being's inordinate desire to out do others for position and prestige is often the root of social impropriety, leading to the neglect of higher values; values by which Allah judges people. The holy Prophet is reported to have said that *Allah does not judge by material wealth nor by external appearance but evaluates each human being according to sincerity of heart and the actions which emanate therefrom.*

We are often reminded in the Qur'an that, *"wealth and progeny are the adornments of this world (which are all temporary), while righteousness and good conduct have permanent positive consequences."* (Q 18:46). In another part of the Qur'an we are reminded that this world is but amusement and play where we adorn ourselves with those things in which we take pride, such as our wealth and our children; but yet again, Allah reminds us; *"O you who believe don't let your wealth and your children divert you from God – consciousness."* (Q 63:9) Therefore, we are advised to love our children and to utilize wealth with due propriety without the world in itself becoming the ultimate object of our existence, nor to over exaggerate the significance of that which is temporary. *"Do not be over amazed by your wealth or your children."* (Q 9:55) *"Take note that your property and your progeny are a means of test for you and surely with Allah is the ultimate reward."* (Q 18:46)

حتى زرتم المقابر
"Until you reach the graveyards."

The glitter and glamour of worldly pleasures and the means through which it is acquired continues to divert many human beings into a false sense of security, until death catches up with them. When people are about to die then they awaken to the reality of life, as the holy Prophet intimated, when he remarked *that people are asleep and when death reaches them, they wake up.*

Allah clearly indicates in the holy Qur'an (18:46) that only our good deeds are of any avail in the after life and as the holy Prophet (pbuh) said: *"A dead person is followed to his grave by three, two of which return and one remains; his relatives, his property and his deeds follow him to the grave; the relatives and property returns, while his deeds remain with him"* (Bukhari). In this is a lesson for those who indulge in improper conduct, engrossing themselves in the world, over – indulging in materialism. Allah warns; *"Shame to every back – biter and slanderer, who amasses wealth, counting it over and over. He thinks that his wealth will immortalize him. Never! such will surely be cast into the crushing torment"* (Q 104:1 – 4).

كلا سوف تعلمون
ثم كلا سوف تعلمون

"But soon will you know, then soon you will know."

Death is a fact of life and as the Qur'an reminds us, *"Every living things must taste death and surely each will then be recompensed on the Day of Resurrection. So whosoever is saved from the fire will be admitted to Paradise, such indeed gain the ultimate goal. And what is the life of this world except a provision of vanity."* (Q 3:184) It must be noted that there is no escape from the reality of death, *"Wherever you are death will surely overtake you"* (Q 4:78).

We note that the verse is repeated and this repetition adds emphasis to (and renders more effective) the warning being announced. This dramatic linguistic style creates an awe – inspiring impact on the heart and mind of the reader and the listener. After the experience of death comes the reality of the afterlife and perhaps the repetition also indicates the awareness created by death followed by the second awareness of the promised accountability leading to success or failure in the Hereafter.

كلا لو تعلمون علم اليقين
"If only you had knowledge of certainty."

The dramatic repetition in the previous verse is followed by a deliberate incomplete verse intended to evoke the conscience of the reader. Most human beings tend to be skeptical about the Hereafter, which implies not taking full cognizance of the reality of eventual accountability for our worldly deeds. If we have a higher degree of consciousness and greater faith in the Truth conveyed to us by the Divine Emissaries, we would have been more aware of the link between our actions in this world and the answerability for them in the Hereafter. It is little wonder that the Prophet Muhammad (pbuh) remarked, *"If you knew what I know, you would laugh less and weep more"* (Bukhari).

لترون الجحيم
"You will surely see the fire."

The fire of hell will be witnessed by everyone, but only the evil will bear the punishment thereof. The Qur'an clearly states that the hell – fire will be shown to all human beings when it says, *"There is none among you but will be brought near to the fire of hell"* (Q 19:71). The Prophet (pbuh) is reported to have said that *no one who enters Paradise will enter without being shown the place he would have occupied in the fire had he been of those who deviated and became corrupted.*

ثم لترونها عين اليقين

"Then you will surely see it with the eye of certainty."

It should be stated here that there are three levels of certainty;
i.) *'Ilm – ul – Yaqeen* (Certainty by Inference). This is not based on direct knowledge but on indirect knowledge; such as when one sees smoke he assumes there to be a fire, but does not see the fire itself.
ii.) *'Ayn – ul – Yaqeen* (Certainty by Sight / direct observation). At this level one sees the fire and this, ofcourse, is a greater degree of certainty than the inference drawn by seeing the smoke. Here one, for example, witnesses the fire.
iii.) *Haqq –ul – Yaqeen* (Certainy by Realization / Experience). When one, for example burns in the fire, he becomes part of the reality. To use another example; one may hear the gushing of water and assume there to be water (*'Ilm – ul – Yaqeen*), thereafter one may see the water confirming that the gushing sound was indeed that of the water (*'Ayn – ul – Yaqeen*). However, when one bathes in the water then he becomes (by experience) at one with the water and this is not by inference, nor observation; but by experience.

So in this verse, we come to the acknowledgement of Truth, with a degree of realization not experienced in this material world and therefore Allah makes reference to witnessing the real experience of the after – life.

ثم لتسئلن يومئذ عن النعيم

"Then, on that Day, you shall be questioned about the favors, bounties and pleasures bestowed upon you."

On the Day of Reckoning, each person will be questioned

about their existence in this world. As the holy Prophet warned, *no person will pass the Day of Judgement without being questioned about his youth and what he did through it, his knowledge and what he did with it, his wealth how he acquired and spent it; and his body how he used or abused it.* The bounties and favors of Allah are immeasurable, as Allah reminds us in the Sacred Book; *"If you were to enumerate the favors of Allah, never would you be able to number them"* (Q 14:34).

The holy Prophet warned that *only those foolish ones hoard for this world who have no real intellect, for only such consider this world as a real abode who have no true abode.* Through Divinely – ordained wisdom, the holy Prophet advised; *"Value five things before five things (come to pass): value your youth before old age arrives, value your health before sickness overtakes you, value your free time before you are overcome with being occupied, value your wealth before poverty siezes you and value your life before death comes"* (*Mustadrak al – Haakim*).

This *surah* calls for great introspection and demands of us to analyze our lives realistically and honestly. *"O you who believe, be sincerely dutiful to Allah and consider what you have sent forth for tomorrow (the future/ the hereafter), and be sincerely dutiful to Allah, for surely Allah is All – Knowing, fully informed."* (Q 59:18) The verse that follows makes reference to those who forget the purpose of life, *"And be not like those who forgot Allah and thereby are caused to forget their own selves. Such are indeed rebellious transgressors."* The resultant reward of the Allah – conscious, who believe and do good deeds, is far different and superior to those who deny the Truth and commit evil. *"Never can you equate the*

93

inhabitants of hell with the inhabitants of Paradise, for surely the inhabitants of Paradise are the triumphantly successful."
(Q 59:20)

We must realize that whatever we have is a gift from Allah and an *amaanah* (trust). The more we have of worldly goods the greater the responsibility we are entrusted with. With knowledge we teach and lead, with wealth we help and relieve, with authority we dispense justice and with faith we manifest goodness. Abuse of any of these is tantamount to the abuse of the *amaanah*. Allah warns those who are blessed, yet fulfill not their obligations, *"you honor not the orphan, nor urge one another to feed the poor, while you devour the heritage of others. You who love wealth with excessive love, do take heed; when the earth is shattered and Divine punishment visits you through angels in ranks, and hell is brought near on that Day; yes, on that Day will you remember (Our Message and Our Warnings), but of what benefit will that remembrance be? Then man will say, how I wish I spent my life doing good which I could have sent forth."*
(Q 89:17 – 24)

From all this, we are bound to acknowledge that the cause of man's downfall and destruction is due to over indulgence in the temporary material things of the world, while true success lies in faith and good deeds which also benefit eternally in the Hereafter. In a *hadith* documented by *Bayhaqi*, the holy Prophet is reported to have recited this *surah* very often and said that it was *equal in value to a thousand verses.*

SURAH AL – IKHLAAS
The Declaration of Allah's Perfection
(Chapter 112)

This *surah* deals with the basic religious belief – unicity of Allah, and has the distinction of being referred to by the Holy Prophet as being *equivalent to one third of the Holy Qur'an* (Sahih Muslim). It is reported that before going to bed *the holy Prophet used to recite this and the last two surahs, at least thrice* (Abu Dawood). This *surah* is entitled *"Ikhlaas"*, (*Sincerity*) because its recitation and deliberation over its subject-matter is calculated to foster in the reader a deep attachment to Allah leading to unwavering sincerity. *Ikhlaas* also means purification from impurity and as this chapter purifies the unity of Allah of all polytheism, it is called *Al-Ikhlaas*.

In view of the importance of its subject matter, the *surah* has come to be known by several names of which some are: *al-Tawhid (Oneness of Allah), al-Ma'rifah (the Knowledge of the Realities), al-Samad (the Absolute)* and *al-Ikhlaas (the Sincerity)*.

Occasion of the revelation of this *Surah*

That this is one of the earliest Makkan *Surahs* is the view of Hasan, 'Ikkrama and, above all, Ibn Masud, (one of the earliest of the Prophet's Companions). Ibn 'Abbas, though much younger than 'Abdullah bin Mas'ud, but regarded as one of the most learned Companions, considers this *surah* to have been revealed at Medinah. In view of the divergent opinions of these two very respected Companions of the holy Prophet, some commentators of the Quran are inclined to think that the *surah* was revealed twice, first at Makkah and then at Medinah.

A narration says that the pagans of Makkah asked a question about the identity of Allah in response to which this *surah* was revealed. In some narrations it is also said that later in Madinah the Christians of Najran asked the same question. There is no contradiction in these narrations because the questions may have been asked by all of them separately, which is in itself, an evidence of the extraordinary importance of this *surah*, answering the questions of different persons from various groups. Historic and contextual evidence however support the idea that this *surah* was revealed in Makkah, and that the holy Prophet also responded to the Christians of Najran by quoting this *surah* later in Medinah.

قل هو الله احد

"Proclaim: He is Allah, the One and Only."

The word "*Qul*" here embodies a command to all Muslims to keep proclaiming "*Allah is One.*"
Thus the term "*Qul*" here, means "*express the fact and tell others.*"
"*Allah*" (*Lafz ul-Jalaalah*) is a proper noun par excellence. No plural can be derived from it and it is according to the best authorities, without derivations. "*Allah*" is the distinctive name for the Supreme Being in the Qur'an. In the Arabic language, the word is never used for any single being. It is a personal name of God, neither attributive nor descriptive.

According to the most correct opinions, *Allah* is the Being who exists necessarily by Himself, comprising all qualities of perfection. The word connotes all the attributes of supremacy, majesty, perfection and beauty in their infinitude and denotes none but the One and Unique God, the Absolute, Supreme, Perfect, Tender, Onmiscient, Onmipresent, Omnipotent, Gracious, Benign and Compassionate. The English word

"God", which is the common Teutonic word for a personal object of religious worship, falls far short in conveying that which is intended by "*ALLAH*".

"*Ahad*" (*the One*) is an epithet applied to Allah alone and signifies, the One; the Sole; He Who has been and will ever be One and Alone; Who has no second to share in His Lordship, nor in His Essence. Allah is One; One in the sense of His Essential Existence, not only in the numerical sense of the word, (which has its second and third), but the One which has no second in an absolute sense. "*One*" beyond dimension, beyond measure and beyond categorization; absolute in essence and manifestation, Unicity of Allah.

الله الصمد

"Allah, the Self-Existing, Eternal, Absolute"

The term "*as-Samad*" occurs in the Qur'an only once, and is applied to Allah alone. It comprises the concepts of *Primary Cause, Eternal, Independent Being*, combined with the idea that everything existing or conceivable goes back to Him as its source and is therefore dependant on Him for its being as well as for its continued existence. In fact, nothing in the universe is complete in itself, not even the smallest atom. Nothing is self-subsisting; everything depends on some other thing for its existence. Allah Alone is such a Being Who depends on no being or thing. He is above conception and conjecture. His attributes are beyond bound or limit. That is the meaning of *as-Samad*.

لم يلد و لم يولد

"He begets not, nor is He begotten"

The Arab pagans believed that angels were the children of Allah. *"...And they falsely, having no knowledge, attribute to Him sons and daughters...,"* (Surah An'am 6:100).

There emitted nothing from Him – neither material things nor a child, nor other things that emit from creatures. The aspect of Divinity can never be reduced to human parenthood or progeny.

و لم يكن له كفوا احد.

"And there is none comparable unto Him"

The Holy Essence of Allah is free from qualities that creatures have; and free from all defects and limitations. This is the Unity of Attributes that corresponds with the Absolute Unicity of the Divine Being.

The fact that Allah is one and unique in every respect, without beginning and without ending, has its logical correlate in the statement that *"there is nothing that could be compared with Him"* – thus precluding any possibility of describing or defining Him. Consequently, the quality of His Being is so sacred that depicting Allah by means of figurative representations or even abstract symbols must be considered as a blasphemous denial of truth and reality.

True Monotheism

This *surah* points out the fundamental errors of many non monotheistic belief systems in its four brief verses:
The first verse proclaims the Unicity of the Divine Being and rejects categorically all forms of polytheism.

In the second verse Allah is said to be "*as-Samad*", which the Holy prophet is reported to have explained as meaning; "*the Lord to Whom recourse is had in every need, so that all have need of Him and He has need of none.*"

The third verse points out the error of those ideologies which describe the Divine literally as Father, Son or Daughter, implying physical familial relationship between the Divine and any creation.

The fourth verse negates such beliefs as incarnation, or doctrines according to which mere human beings are likened to God.

Thus the four kinds of Shirk are rejected here; a belief in the plurality of gods (v.1), a belief that other things possess the perfect attributes of the Divine Being (v.2), a belief that God is either a Father or a Son (v.3), and a belief that others can do that which is ascribable only to Allah or that anything is comparable to Him (v.4).

SURAH AL – BALAD
THE CITY
CHAPTER 90

لا اقسم بهذا البلد

"I swear by the City" or *"I call to attention by the City."*

The *surah* opens with a forceful, assertive oath, pertaining to the **City of Makkah** and is the word from which the *surah* takes its tittle. This city is a valley surrounded by mountains. A city which is barren, has no water of its own, no cultivable land, situated in the desert where the climate is very harsh. The geographical location and historical condition of the city brings to our attention the fact that this world is not meant to be a place for ease but a place for striving and labor, a place for testing human beings; for life itself is a test, as the Qur'an brings to our attention in *surah al – Mulk* verse 3;
"Allah created death and life in order that He may test you in this world, through your deeds."

The very fact that Adam and Houwa (peace be upon them) are said to have met at 'Arafah in the vicinity of Makkah indicates that from the outset, life was not specifically meant to be lived luxuriously. We also notice that the city of Makkah is the region which Allah selected for the construction of His "house". Behind the selection there is perchance a hidden wisdom, that those who eventually would go on pilgrimage; as millions do today, should be drawn by its internal beauty and not its apparent harshness.

By swearing an oath, attention is drawn to this city of Makkah, a city of which the Prophet (pbuh) said: "*I swear by Allah, that this part of the earth of Allah is more beloved to Allah than any other part of the world; and I swear by Allah, if I was not made to leave thee, I would not have left*" (Tirmidhi) (Musnad of Ahmad Ibn Hanbal).

و انت حل بهذا البلد

After making reference to the city of Makkah which contains the sacred house of Allah, the first place ever to be erected on earth as a place of worship where people put down their weapons and meet in harmony, a place of peace, a place of sanctity and sacredness, Allah then mentions;

"*(O Muhammad) you are hillum in this city*" (verse 2). It could imply that the holy Prophet (pbuh) is the *one who abides by the law*, for **hillum** could mean *doing what is lawful*. **Hillum** can also imply *a target* meaning Muhammad (pbuh) is the target of every conceivable harm, cruelty, injury and abuse against his honor and his life. As we know, he experienced hardship and opposition to the extent that he had to migrate in the 52nd year of his life from Makkah, (the city of his birth), to (Yathrib) Madinah. It also implies *freedom from obligation* and as we know the Rasul (pbuh) re-entered the city victoriously, alighting as a conqueror (in 8 *Hijrah*), driving out; by the command of Allah, all forms of abominations, evil, corruption and falsehood; without perpetrating any atrocities. In the words of famous historian and writer, Dr. Stanley Lane – Poole; "*The day of Muhammad's greatest triumph over his enemies was the day of his grandest victory... The army followed his example and entered quietly and peacefully. No house was robbed, no women insulted. One thing alone suffered destruction; going to the Ka'bah, Muhammad stood before each of the 360 idols and pointed to them with his staff saying: "truth has arrived and falsehood shall perish, for* *falsehood by its very nature is bound to perish." At these words his attendants hewed the idols down... It was thus that Muhammad entered his native city. Through all annals of conquests there is no triumphant entry comparable to this one."*

و والد وما ولد

After swearing an oath by the city and bringing to our attention the significance of the city of *Makkah* and the fact that the *Rasul* is a dweller in that city, Allah says; *"By the father and the son, By the parent and the child"* (verse 3). This indicates continuation of the Adamic thread and the perpetuation of humanity. Adam was the first (prototype) of human beings and we are all human beings like him.

There could also be reference to Ibrahim (pbuh) and his son Ismail (pbuh), for when Ibrahim was busy raising the foundation of and rebuilding the *Ka'bah*, he, together with his son, prayed the following words which are documented in Qur'an 2, verse 130; *"O Lord, raise amongst them a Messenger from among themselves who may recite to them Thy signs and teach them the Book and the Wisdom and perchance purify them."* So the expression *the father and the son* may refer to Ibrahim and Ismail, and of course, Ismail was the great forefather of Prophet Muhammad (pbut).

We note here that after making reference to the honorable position of the city of *Makkah* as having hosted the final Divine Messenger, we are made aware that the city has received an added sanctity by being the sanctuary in which Prophet Muhammad was born and eventually to which he returned victorious, as the leader of the People of Faith; removing from it falsehood and idolatry, until the Day of *Qiyamah*.

لقد خلقنا الانسان فى كبد

"We have certainly created the human being to toil and strive."

This implies that human beings are in toil from the beginning to the end and that life and all that it contains are a series of trials and tribulations, joy and sorrow, happiness and tears; combinations which we have to endure with patient perseverance and with faith, in order to succeed, to deserve the eternal bliss of the Hereafter. We are also requested to strive throughout our life in the path of Allah, as the Qur'an says; *"Whoever strives towards Us, We shall guide them to Our ways."*

Allah's swearing by parent and child draws our attention to the great importance of the stage of reproduction in life and to the invincible wisdom and perfection which this stage involves. It also envisages the great striving and patience endured by parent and off – spring from conception up to maturity.

ايحسب ان لن يقدر عليه احد
يقول اهلكت مالا لبدا
ايحسب ان لم يره احد

Does the human being think that no one has power over him because he has at his disposal enormous amounts of material wealth. "Does the human being think that no one sees him?"

The surah here discusses the behavior of many human beings who very often forget the real nature and purpose of life and

103

the eventual answerability for their deeds; becoming conceited with their status, wealth and authority. They neglect their responsibility, abuse power, ability and skill which Allah had given them and use these in a manner as if oblivious to their accountability to anyone. They indulge in oppression, victimization, exploitation, tyranny, injustice; all these in order to acquire material wealth and status; in the process corrupting others as well. Such are reminded that Allah is ever watchful over them. The abundance of *lubadaa* (implying material posession) in the hands of one who does not consider that it would ever be exhausted, lives as if this world is his final abode. The holy Prophet (pbuh) made reference to those who are so materialistically inclined by saying that *the world is considered the abode for one who has no real abode and therefore those who hoard for this world have no real sense of intelligence.*

The consequence of such careless thinking results in irresponsible attitudes. They are those who make their wealth a means of exhibition, of wasteful spending, of corrupting and undermining others; failing to solve the basic (economic and social) problems that many suffer.

الم نجعل له عينين
و لسانا و شفتين

"Have We not given him two eyes, a tongue and two lips."

Here Allah makes reference to the fact that He has granted human beings the faculty of speech and the means of expression; the faculty of sight and observation. These are favors (*ni'mah*) bestowed on human beings in order to aid them in following the Path of Guidance. The eyes with which we can recognize the evidence of Allah's Might and His

Majesty manifested throughout the universe, prompting him to be faithful. His tongue and lips (faculty of speech) is a means of expression and communication.

After consciously witnessing with the eyes, a sense of gratitude should originate in the heart and be expressed through lips. Some consider that the two eyes refer to different levels of vision, one is sight and the other is insight. Some say the eyes refer to the physical eye and the spiritual eye, the inner eyes of the *Ruh* or the *Qalb* (the eye of the soul or the eye of the heart) as different from the material eye.

وهديناه النجدين

"And We have pointed out to them the two ways."

The two ways could be the distinctly opposite ways of virtue and vice; the *Tariq as – Salih* and the *Tariq al – Kharaab* (which is the path of righteousness and the path of ruination). Some say it refers to the path of basic belief of the *Muslim* and the other the path of full expression of the practicality of Faith of the *Mu'min*. The *Muslim* is basically one who testifies to faith in word and fulfills his ritual obligations, while a *Mu'min* is one who comprehensively manifest faith in thought, word and deed.

Some say the two paths refer to the path of the *Shari'ah* (the legalistic aspect of the path of faith) and the other is the *Tariqah* (the spiritual dimension), the latter being completely in the ambit of the former.

فلا اقتحم العقبة
وما ادراك ما العقبة

Allah then makes reference to the practical expression of faith which goes beyond mere belief and mere ritual and perchance the reference here is to the *Tariqah* of the *Mu'min*, Allah says; *"But they do not choose the uphill path, and what shall indicate to you what the uphill path is?"* (verses 9 – 10) *'Aqabah* implies a difficult course which passes between mountains and if one wants to traverse this path, one has to climb steep highways. Spiritually, it may refer to the path of righteousness. As we know Jesus / 'Isa (pbuh) is reported to have said in the <u>Book of Mathew</u>, Chapter 7, verse 13; *"Enter by the narrow gate for the gate that is wide and the way easy, many enter it; as for the gate that is narrow and the way hard, that leads to life and those who find it are few."*

What should one do to attain access to the uphill path?

فك رقبة

او اطعام في يوم ذي مسغبة

يتيما ذا مقربة

او مسكينا ذا متربة

"The uphill path is traversed by the freeing of the one who is in bondage or the feeding of the hungry at a time of need whether it be an orphan who is near – of – kin or a poor person lying in the dust."

Here Allah makes reference to social welfare and its link with faith, for mere lip-service is not sufficient. *Imaan* needs to be coupled with *'aml al- salihat – (faith expressed through good actions).* Good deeds incorporate actions for the benefit of humanity at large and therefore it begins by saying that to traverse the uphill path *"fakkurakabah"* one must free those who are in bondage, those who are suffering any form of subjugation and exploitation, whether it be social, religious, economic, moral or political; for all of these are forms of bondage.

In feeding the poor, it is not sufficient to feed at whim and fancy (in accordance with one's moods) but rather to meet the needs of the time and one should consider specifically those who are deprived (like the orphans and the oppressed). Charity should begin at home. Help those within your family who are neglected and those closest to you. We should not be of those who overlook the poor and helpless, those who are deserving of our help in every condition; including those who lie filthy in the dust, they are part of our society, part of the progeny of Adam, our brothers and sisters in humanity and our responsibility. Be not oblivious to the realities and suffering of the majority and realize that whatever we have is purely a trust from the Creator and the more we have the more we are answerable, the more we are responsible. The more we have, the more we can assist others. The idea is to evoke in the Believers a sense of mercy, of sympathy, of co-operation, of selflessness and affection.

These good deeds must not be the result of a momentary impulse. The desire to assist should not be motivated by any social reputation, name, fame or self – interest. Furthermore, in keeping up with the prophetic spirit of the one who cared for the orphans, liberator of slaves, the defender of women, and the protector of the oppressed and the down – trodden; Muhammad (pbuh) instructed us that *Allah is at the assistance of his servant as long as that servant is at the assistance of his fellow human beings.* In another hadith, this greatest exemplar is reported to have said *that all creation is part of the family of*

Allah and the most loved of all people to Allah are those who are best to Allah's universal family."

We can see that Islam has placed a tremendous emphasis on the need for the upliftment of the poor and the deprived. No wonder the following verse reads;

ثم كان من الذين امنوا

"Then are you of those who truly Believe"; indicating that mere proclamation of faith and basic rituals are not sufficient, only after manifesting that belief in beneficial action which has a positive effect in society, can one truly say *"I am of those who truly have faith."*

و تواصوا با لصبر وتواصوا بالمرحمة
اولئك اصحاب الميمنة

"Exhort one another to patient perseverance and exhort one another to compassion and mercy. Such are the people of the right hand."

Doing good is not sufficient for raising the all – round structure and improving the lot of the community. Good ideals and proper principles combined with continuous sustained adherence to the path of economic, spiritual and moral rectitude; teaching of virtues, encouraging and consoling others are all equally essential for the attainment of social upliftment. We are not asked to only be patient and merciful but also to be of those who engender the spirit of mercy by exhorting others to be merciful and creating the conditions for mercy to be manifested and for patient perseverance to be exercised. We should have close co –

operation with each other in creating a platform for sympathetic well – wishing whenever the need arises and never leave those who are deprived or distressed to themselves; forsaken and neglected.

The *"people of the right hand"* are the people of correct action, of proper faith and are of those who are destined for the Garden of Eternal Bliss in the Hereafter.

و الذين كفروا بايتنا هم اصحاب المشئمة
عليهم نار مؤصدة

"Those who disbelieve in our signs they are the people of the left hand, such will be engulfed by flames."

Here Allah makes reference to those who act in opposition to the Truth and live oblivious to the reality. They are warned about the blazing fire which would be their lot.

It is significant to note that reference is made in this early Makkan *surah* to social upliftment, economic and moral well – being. This, at a time when the Prophet, his companions and family were being suppressed at this early stages of his mission. The essentials of Faith, the building block of Islam, the foundation of Islam was laid at that period, and social welfare clearly seems to have been a top priority. Allah, in His infinite wisdom, found it necessary (even then) to link up social welfare and moral rectitude with the basics of the Faith. It makes one ponder on the fact that social welfare is inextricably interlinked with personal rectitude and spiritual development in Islam.

SURAH AL-FATIHAH
THE OPENING
(CHAPTER 1)

The *Basmalah* or *Tasmiyah*

بسم الله الرحمان الرحيم

"In the Name of Allah, The Beneficent, Most Merciful."

After attestation to Faith (*Shahaadah*), the most cardinal and often used formula is *BISMILLA – HIR – RAHMA – NIR – RAHIM*. The invocation (*al-Basmalah*) has from the beginning occupied an important and special place in Muslim piety and practices.

Purpose of *Basmalah*

Of the many good practices instituted by Islam is that Muslims should begin all their activities in the Name of Allah. Remembering the Name of Allah before starting any act is an admission on the part of the actor that everything is the creation of Allah and that whatever activity or skill is to be exercised, has been granted by Allah; thus developing a degree of proprietal consciousness and a sense of gratitude to the Creator. If the *Basmalah* is thus consciously applied it could restrain wrongful conduct; since one in his right mind would not pronounce the Name of Allah and then commit evil, indecency or wrongful acts. In this way, illegitimate activity would be avoided, thus ensuring that the initiation of deeds and the doer's mental orientation are good. In addition to that, when a person reads the *Basmalah*, the Name of Allah is

110

invoked and due to Allah's nobility, perfection, grandeur and sanctity, the activity which follows are Divinely blessed, protected from evil and thus sanctified.

Place of *Basmalah*

Scholars are agreed on the following:
The *Basmalah* is a verse of the Qur'an
It is part of a verse of *Surah Naml* (27:30)
It is not part of the ninth chapter (*Surah Taubah*)
It is part of *Surah al-Fatihah* according to all seven *Imaams* of *Qira'ah* (i.e. *Imaams 'Aasim, Kisa'ie, Nafi', Abu 'Amru, Ibn 'Aamir, Ibn Katheer and Hamzah*) and according to the *Mathaahieb* (schools of jurisprudence) of *Shaf'ie, Zaydi, Zahiri, 'Ibadie* and *Ja'farie.*
The *Hanafi, Maliki* and *Hanbali* schools differ with this view.

Importance of *Basmallah*

The Qur'an documents its first revelation as: "*Read! In the Name of thy Rabb Who Created*" (Alaq 96:1). In the old Testament (Duet 18:18), we read "*I will raise them (the Semites) a Prophet from among their brethren, like unto thee (Moses) and I will put my words in his mouth, and he shall speak unto them all that I shall command him. And it shall come to pass that whosoever will not hearken unto my words which he shall speak in My Name, and I will require it from him.*"
As the holy Prophet of Islam was raised in the likeness of Moses (Q 73:16), so in fulfillment of the above prophecy, Allah so ordained that each time a new *surah* was revealed, it was begun by the words; **In the Name of Allah, the Beneficent, Most Merciful.**

111

The holy Prophet Muhammad (pbuh) is reported to have said *that any action of importance not begun with Basmalah is devoid of blessing and therefore incomplete.* The *Basmalah* begins the *Surah al-Fatihah* and therefore opens the whole Qur'an.

The Almighty describes Himself by means of His Attributes. The Attributes of Allah are a means of us becoming knowledgeable about Him. Allah, in this respect, does not only introduce the Qur'an but He also introduces Himself. The *Basmalah* is an invocation of the Divine being by His supreme Name (Allah), followed by two of His most beautiful names (*Ar-Rahman Ar-Rahim*), which are in fact two of His principal Divine attributes. This headline, introduction or foreword called the *Basmalah*, encapsulates in one brief sentence the Creator's relation to creation – the relation of love, care, concern, sympathy, compassion and mercy.

Bismillah literally means ***"In the Name of Allah"***, ***"By the Name of Allah"***, ***"via the Assistance and Blessing Of the One called Allah."***

The three parts to this phrase are **B**, **Ism** and **Allah**.
"**B**" could mean "in", "by" or "through".
"**Ism**" means name. Names are given to objects in order to provide them with a sign by which they may be recognized and distinguished from other things. When the word "Ism" is used in relation to the Creator, it implies an inherent Divine Attribute. According to the Quran (59:24; 17:110), unto Allah belongs the most Beautiful Names (*Asma-ul-Husna*) and according to prophetic Tradition, Allah has 99 Names. These attributes and Names are of paramount importance since we know the Divine Being through them. It must be noted that no Name or attribute of the Almighty is in contradistinction to

another of His attributes or Names. He is Compassionate with all of His being, Merciful with all of His being, Light with all of His being; thus the essence of His many perfect attributes are not separate from one another. All His Names and attributes participate in all degree of His being through the unicity of His Essence. His Holy Names represent reflections of the reality of His Sacred Essence.

"*Allah*" – This word is a proper noun par excellence. Neither diminutive nor plural can be formed from it. It denotes all attributes of perfection in their infinitude and refers to none other than the Absolute One, the Unique, Self-subsisting and Supreme Being. The word "*Allah*" is thus the most comprehensive Name of the Divine Being.

Both the words **Rahman** and **Rahim** are derived from the root *RHM* which signifies tenderness, care, consideration, affection – requiring the exercise of beneficence, goodness, love, compassion, benevolence and mercy. Allah says in the Qur'an, "*My Rahmah encompasses everything*" (7:155). To indicate the intensity and comprehensiveness of the Mercy of Allah, two intensive forms of the word *Rahmah* are used side by side and in *Surah al-Fatihah* it is repeated in the third verse as an independent *aayah* (**Ar-Rahman-ir-Raheem**). As a matter of fact, no other attribute of Allah has so often been stressed in the Holy Book (over 300 times) than this Divine attribute of *Rahmah*.

At the very threshold of one's study of the Sacred Scripture, one is ushered into the awareness of the Creator and made conscious of His Holy Presence and reminded of His boundless Grace and limitless Mercy.

The *Basmallah* introduces the "Opening of the Book" (*Al-Fatihah*) and thus marks the inauguration of the Final Divine Communiqué – the Holy Qur'an.

الحمد لله

"All praise is due to Allah"

There are basically four words in the Arabic language, which are used in varying degrees to signify thankfulness, adoration and praise. These are *shukr, thanaa', madh* and *hamd.*

Shukr expresses recognition of benefits, gratitude and thankfulness for favors received. *Thanaa'* denotes repetitive public acknowledgements. *Madh* means adoration. *Hamd* is neither pure *madh* (praise) for *madh* can be false; nor simply *shukr* (gratitude) but rather more than a combination of both. *Hamd* implies admiration, sincere adoration and heartfelt gratitude, expressed with humility. *Hamd* can therefore not be directed to any other than Allah.

The definite article *Al* prefixed to *Hamd* and the preposition *Li* before *Allah* emphasizes the fact that all forms of praise, adoration, gratitude and thanks in the true sense is due solely to Allah. The word *Hamd* is thus the most appropriate word to be used here since the reference is to the intrinsic grandeur, goodness and truly merited praise, adoration and glorification of the Supreme Being (Allah).

Al-Hamdu lillah implies the magnifying, glorifying, honoring and recognizing the supremacy and majesty of Allah combined with humility and submissiveness of the person who offers the *hamd.*

It is also significant to note that we are not made to say, "I praise Allah"; because if we were to praise Allah thus, it would limit the extent of the *hamd* according to the individual's limited perception. *Al-Hamdu lillah* conveys the expression of praise to the One worthy of praise at all times, under all circumstances and independently of the individual's imperfect realization of Allah.

Realizing that *Hamd* may be rendered in word, thought, deed and spiritual state; it is however verbally expressed by a Muslim on a worthy achievement, on completion of a task or expressing one's physical condition.

The phrase *Al-Hamdu lillah* is of such great significance that after the *Basmalah* and the *Shahadah*, (attestation to Faith), it is the third most commonly used phrase in the Muslim world. In this *surah*, *Al-Hamdu lillah* is the complement of *Basmalah*. *Al-Hamdu lillah* ends and act as *Basmalah* begins and initiates the act. As the *Basmalah* develops in one degree of proprietal consciousness, ensuring that the actor's mental and spiritual orientation are good and sound; *Al-Hamdu lillah* integrates the positive content of the act with consciousness of the fact that whatever the person does that is admirable, (in essence) comes from the blessings and bounty of Allah – the source of ultimate goodness and perfection.

As it would be ethically improper to invoke Allah's Name on beginning something wrongful and sinful, so too the *Hamd*, for it can not be integrated except after an act that is good, wholesome, beneficial and pleasing to Allah. All this imprints positively on one's soul the criterion and spiritual value of an act. So, *Al-Hamdu lillah* means that *ultimately, all forms and degrees of any expression of praise, together with the very essence and notion of praise, belongs solely to Allah.*

رب العلمين

"The Rabb of all the worlds."

The word **Rabb** implies *Lord and Master*; *Ruler and Sovereign*; *Facilitator of development of inherent aptitudes*; *Sustainer, Provider, Cherisher, Nourisher* and *Guardian*.

'Aalameen applies to all created things, all categories of beings and everything other than Allah. The expression **Rabbil 'Aalameen** is significant for at least two reasons:

1. It serves as a declaration that this Qur'an (from the outset) obliterates the false notion that Allah is a partial God. There is only One worthy of worship who is also the Creator of all and Whose guidance is universal; so too is the content of this Holy Book which refers to Allah at its opening as **Rabbul 'Aalameen**.

2. By linking **Al-Hamdu lillah** with **Rabbil 'Aalameen**, our attention is drawn to the fact that we as Muslims are part of a wider world which is multi-dimensional, all of which Allah is equally the Lord and Master.

It also brings to our attention the universality of the message of the Qur'an and that true Believers are supposed to be concerned about the welfare of all that which Allah cares for. Was it not the holy Prophet Muhammad (pbuh) who so aptly said: *"All creation is part of the family of Allah and Allah loves most those who are most beneficial to His universal family."*

116

الرحمان الرحيم

"The Beneficent, Most Merciful."

In the first verse of *Al-Fatihah*, the attributes of **Rahmaan** and **Raheem** serve as a key to this chapter. Here in the third verse it is used as a link between the attributes of *Rabb-ul-Alameen* and *Maliki Yawmiddeen* (between Facilitator of development and the Just Sovereign).

The words **Rahmaan** and **Raheem** are both derived from **Rahmat (mercy)**. *Rahmah* combines the idea of *riqqah* (tenderness) and *ihsaan* (goodness). Its connotation is wide enough to incorporate the qualities of love, benevolence, generosity and compassion. The two superlatives ***Ar-Rahman*** and ***Ar-Raheem***, which express intensive *Rahmah*, denotes different dimensions of Allah's mercy.

Ar-Rahman pertains to Allah's all inclusive expression of mercy which He shows and bestows on all creation extensively and gratuitously, without regard to effort, by providing the necessary means, faculties and facilities for reaching the highest stage of fulfillment and development. Scholars concur that the word *Rahman* is reserved for Allah alone and there is no plural for the word *Rahman*.

Ar-Raheem refers to Allah's perennial expression of mercy which manifests itself in the form of eternal blessings and reward as a consequence of efforts and good deeds. *Ar-Raheem* in actual fact signifies that when means and faculties bestowed on human beings are appropriately and effectively utilized, Allah eternally rewards the person.
It appears that the purpose of the Holy Qur'an bringing to the attention of the reader *Ar-Rahman* and *Ar-Raheem*

simultaneously, is perchance to emphasize the all – embracing *Rahmah* of Allah.

Of all the attributes of Allah, the Qur'an has made more reference to His *Rahmah* than to any of His other noble and perfect attributes.

ملك يوم الدين

"The Ultimate Authority on the Day of Requital."

The attribute of Allah which the Qur'an mentions in continuation of its reference to *Rub-ub-iyyah* and *Rahmah* is that of *'Adalah* (Justice). The verse *Maaliki Yawmid-Deen* bears the meaning of, *"He Who is the Dispenser of ultimate Justice on the Day of Requital."* It refers to the fundamental teaching of Islam pertaining to the concept of resurrection and retribution.

The Holy Qur'an facilitates the readings *"Maaliki "* and *"Maliki."* Amongst the Quraa', Imaams 'Asim and Kisa'ie read *"Maaliki"* whereas the rest of the seven Quraa' (Imaams Nafi', Abu 'Amru, Ibn Katheer, Hamza and Ibn 'Aamir) read *"Maliki."* *"Malik"* means king, ruler or sovereign and *"Maalik"* means master or one who possesses ownership.

The use of the concept *Maalik / Malik* serves a dual purpose. It firstly encourages a person; who due to human frailty may have committed a sin, not to despair; because Allah the All Merciful, has the capacity and power to forgive. Secondly, it serves as a warning against taking undue advantage of Allah's mercy, for He has the right and authority to punish the wicked. So this verse inspires the reader or the listener with both hope

118

in Allah's Beneficence and fear of Allah's punishment; and this balance is essential for the moral and spiritual development and progress of human beings.

"*Yawm*" could imply time, a day, a portion of a day (from sunrise to sunset), the present... When we consider the usage of "*Yawm*" in the Qur'an we have to appreciate it in the context in which it appears, for it has been used to express various periods of time (see Qur'an 5:4; 22:8; 32:5; 55:29; 70:4). Here in this verse, it refers to the resurrection and the period of accountability that will follow it.

The belief in the Hereafter and the Final Judgment motivates a person to organize and orientate his life in a certain way; rendering his dues to the Creator and fulfilling his obligations and responsibility towards the rest of creation. According to the Holy Qur'an, everyone is to be held accountable on (*Yawmiddeen*) Day of Judgement, whosoever has fulfilled his earthly responsibilities will then be eternally successful.

The word "*Deen*" could mean ... way of life, framework for governance, recompense, reward, requital, judgement, dominion, obedience or religion. The word has been used in the Holy Qur'an in all these senses (see 4:126; 5:4; 12:77; 24:3; 37:54)

The emphasis on Divine authority at the Final Judgement is perhaps to distinguish the mundane and incomplete judgements, rewards and punishments of rulers and superiors in this world from the exclusive and absolute recompense of the Almighty, which reaches fulfillment and completion in the Hereafter. The mastery, kingdom and authority will on that day exclusively be Allah's (22:56-57; 82:18-19). Thus, on the Day of Judgement, the reckoning will be exact, complete, final and absolute; free from error and without undue punishment. No injustice will be done to anyone and every injustice experienced in this world will be fully remedied.

The order in which the four Divine characteristics, *RABBUL'AALAMEEN, AR-RAHMAN, AR-RAHEEM* and *MAALIKI YAWMIDDEEN* appear, indicates how Allah manifests His attributes. After reference to the all-encompassing and comprehensive Mercy in the *Basmalah*, His attribute of being *Lord of all Existence* manifests itself, implying that together with the creation of the human being, Allah creates the necessary environment for his material and spiritual progress. Through the attribute of *Most Gracious* does Allah provide the means required to attain fulfillment and when appropriate use has been made of the faculties and facilities thus provided, the perennial expression of Allah's being *Most Merciful* manifests itself. The collective result of human labor and endeavor are then remunerated by the *absolute authority on the Day of Retribution.*

MAALIKI YAWMIDDEEN brings to light the fact that the sustenance and guidance for human being are gifts from Allah; but the success achieved and recompense received is subject to the deeds one performs.

اياك نعبد

"Thee alone do we worship,"

Though this entire *surah* is considered to be a prayer, this verse is the beginning of the supplication proper.

Allah is spoken of in the first four verses in the third person, but in this (the fifth verse) He is directly addressed in the second person. Thoughtful contemplation of the four previous verses create in a person such an attraction to and an irresistible longing for the Creator that to satisfy this desire for Divine proximity the direct address is used.

Iyyaka (Thee alone) appears before the plural verbs *Na'budu (we worship)* and *Nasta'een (we seek assistance)* in order to emphasize and stress the fact that Allah alone is deserving of worship and Allah is truly the source of aid and succour. The phrase *Iyyaka Na'budu* implies "**only You we worship and no one else but You**." Like the *Kalimah "La ilaha illa Allah"*, this phrase also conveys affirmation and negation; negation of worshipping other that Allah and affirmation of servitude only to the Supreme.

Na'budu (we worship) is derived from *'Abd. 'Ibadah* is the noun infinitive from *'Abd* and signifies adoration, humility, obedience, submissiveness, worship and servitude to the Supreme Being. In the context of this verse *'Ibadah* carries all these meanings simultaneously. It must be borne in mind that *'Ibaadah* in Islam does not imply merely acts of ritual worship. *'Ibaadah* is the symbol, expression and manifestation of the will to obey Allah and includes all actions done in obedience to Him and encompasses all good and beneficial deeds.

"*You do we worship*" expresses exclusivity and completeness of orientation and makes transition from praise, Divine mercy, Divine dominion and ownership previously referred to into acknowledgement of subjection to the One worthy of worship. These opening verses of *al-Fatihah* envision the entire universe as filled with Allah's attributes. There is nothing

121

really to sense but His creation which is a manifestation of His all-pervading existence; nothing to experience but attraction to Him, drawing nearer to Him, tearing apart all bonds of servitude to other than Him. *"You alone (O Allah) do we worship."*

وإياك نستعين

"And Thee alone (O Allah), Do We Beseech For Help"

The mental attitude evoked by this phrase is that of dependence on Allah. Not only do we worship Allah but our relationship with Him is such that we turn to Him for assistance. Recognizing Allah as the Lord of all existence and Master of all blessings and benefactions, we turn to Him in search of fulfillment of our needs, to Whom we stretch forth our hands in supplication and in Whom we repose our trust.

This consciousness of a person's absolute dependence upon Allah indicates the attitude of resignation that a true Believer ought to have. This dependence and resignation has nothing to do with despondence and despair, rather it illuminates hope out of conviction that the Being who is Supreme Lord of the whole universe is powerful enough to help and save one in the most trying circumstances, if we patiently persevere.

This prayerful phrase is a logical corollary to the previous phrase for it is rightful and appropriate to seek help only from the One Whom the individual refers to as his *Rabb* and Whom he has vowed to worship exclusively.

It is significant to note that the plural from of *Na'budu (we worship)* and *Nasta'een (we seek assistance)* has been used. This clearly indicates that the life-values in Islam are permeated with the spirit of social fellowship. The pledge of worship as well as the request for help are not in a person's individual capacity but from and on behalf of all collectively.

Here we are taught to beg Allah with full consciousness of human brotherhood and a desire for salvation of the entire humanity. One should not be concerned only with one's own self as it could tantamount to egotism, pride and arrogance. The pronoun *"we"* here negates selfish individuality as the *'aabid* (worshipper) includes himself in the multitude of humanity, removing egoism, creating humility and effacing the tendency of self-importance.

When we analyze *Surah al-Fathiha*, we find reference to the grandeur of Allah in the first four verses. The last two verses pertain to the aspiration of human soul to attain spiritual loftiness. The verse *Iyyaka Na'budu wa Iyyaka Nasta'een* refers to the relation of the human spirit to the Divine and attaining felicity through *'Ibaadah* (obedience combined with humility) and *Isti'aanah* (soliciting Divine help unselfishly). Through this verse we acknowledge our relationship with Allah and actually commit ourselves thus...

O Allah! We bow down to Your laws for the development of our potentialities, by using our capabilities for the benefit of humanity and all existence; we seek Your help in shaping our lives within Your prescribed pattern and though all human being may not realize Your grandeur and Your being worthy of worship, on behalf of those of us who do worship You we beseech Your assistance for all, after all Your are...

Allah (the Supreme Being),

Rabb-ul-'Aalameen (Facilitator of development for all existence),

Ar-Rahman-ir-raheem (the Beneficient, Most Merciful),

Maalik/Malik-I-yawm-id-Deen (Master and King of the period of Recompense;
therefore *Iyyaka Na'budu wa Iyyaka Nasta-een).*

Some scholars consider this verse to be the epitome of the *Fatihah.*

اهدنا الصراط المستقيم
"Guides us (on to) the Right Path"

The word *Hidayah* and its derivatives are generally used in three senses:
1. To show the right path
2. To lead to the right path
3. To make one follow the right way.

The Qur'an has used the word in all three senses in *Surahs Al-Balad* (9:11), *Al-'Ankabut* (29:70) and *Al-a'raf* (7:44) respectively. The word *Ihdina (guide us)* here is certainly of the widest application and signifies the soul's inner desire to be shown and conveyed to the best of destinations. *Ihdina* is a loving and humble request for perfect guidance (from the Divine) towards the ultimate goal.

Grades of Guidance

The Holy Qur'an, in *surah Al-a'la* (87:2-3), makes reference to four different stages in the process of Divine creative activity:
1. *Takhleeq* – Allah brings to existence the previously non-existent
2. *Taswiyah* – fashioning the created being in a form appropriate to its level of existence

3. *Taqdir* – assigning to the creation an appropriate role and imbuing it with ability consistent with its form
4. *Hidayah* – to show it the natural way for its existence and development through inherent and external modes of guidance.

Hidayah has been provided as a gift of nature. The Holy Qur'an states:
"Our Provider is He Who granted everything a particular nature then provided it with appropriate guidance."
(Taha 20:50)

It is due to the inherent *Hidayah* that various animate and inanimate components are able to perform functions peculiarly entrusted to it. In general significance, *Hidayah* is common to all creation including matter, plants and animals, because according to the Holy Qur'an (*Al-Isra'* 17:44), each category of creation has its own level of consciousness.

There exist basically four grades of *Hidayah*:
1. *Hidayah of instinct* which serve as inspiration and tends to be intuitive.
2. *Hidayah of the senses* which provides those sectors of creation which have the sensory faculties of touch, taste, smell, sight, and hearing to gather information of the external world and react and interact upon that sensory information.
3. *Hidayah of reason* is that directive force inherent in human beings, which suggests the manner instinctive and sensory information could be utilized to open endless vistas of development.
4. *Al-Hidayah* (the Ultimate Guidance). In keeping with Allah's *Rububiyyah* and *Rahmah*, He has throughout history granted us Divine Guidance via Revelation. This

125

level of guidance is probably the greatest Divine gift vouchsafed to humanity as the Holy Qur'an constantly asserts: *"We have created human beings from the union of sexes that We might test him; We granted him sensory faculties and provided him the Guidance to the Right Path; whether he be thankful or ungrateful."* (*Al-Insan* 76:2-3). Therefore we are instructed: *"Say, certainly the Guidance from Allah is the Ultimate Guidance."* (*Al-An'am* 6:71)

History bears testimony to the fact that the only Revelation that has come down to us preserved in its pristine pure form is... *"the Revelation, al-Qur'an, a source of Guidance for all humanity."* (*Al-Baqarah* 2:185)

The Straight Path

In common usage, **Sirat** means a *pathway which can be trodden by the general public without difficulty.* Human beings possess a variety of conflicting propensities and must choose their way from among these. There are innumerable ways, but only *Al – Sirat* leads to the ultimate destination. A person is free to choose but must be prepared to bear the consequences of his choice. When we analyze the Holy Qur'an we find that the opposite of *Truth* or of the Right Path is referred to as *"Zulumaat"* which is always in the plural form. This implies that the ways of deviation and corruption are many while the way of Allah is one; *Siratul Mustaqim*. This does not negate the fact that there are, however, various approaches to Allah, each differing from the other depending on nearness or remoteness of the person from the reality and the individual's level of honesty, sincerity, purity and consciousness.

The word *Al – Mustaqeem* means *undeviating, straight and*

rightly-directed. **Siratul Mustaqim** is thus that path which, by following, one incurs Allah's pleasure. It never fails to guide and leads the wayfarer to his/ her coveted destination. It must be acknowledged that in Islamic philosophy, all worldly and heavenly affairs are exclusively manifest in the phrase *the Right Path*, which leads to the very object of existence in this world and the Hereafter. Thus, the *Straight Path* does not confine itself to mean only doctrines or ritual observances but addresses all dimension of human existence.

It often sarcastically stated that Muslims offer this prayer because they have not yet found the *Straight Path*. On the contrary, this verse teaches one to pray, not only for Allah to show him the *Right Path*, nor merely to lead him to the *Right Path*; but that the Almighty may enable the beseecher to remain guided. As long as we have requirements unfulfilled, goals unattained and needs unsatisfied; we stand in need of this most comprehensive and apt prayer.

The *Straight Path* is not created through conflict or association between opposites as claimed by Dialecticians. The Path has direction from the very outset. Contrary to the theory of the

Existentialists who claim that there is neither way nor destination nor value but these are inventions of man to deal with the uncertain. In Islam we believe that the way to perfection is by treading the *Straight Path*, and is a journey to be experienced rather than invented.

Siratal Mustaqim is the path that keeps the wayfarer from excess, raises him above sin and corruption, makes him **Mustaqim** (steadfast) in this world and leads to paradise in the Hereafter. Owing to the oneness of intelligence and the intelligible, the road and the wayfarer become one

(*Mustaqim*); each objective becomes a new beginning leading to a higher consciousness; each new idea and intention leads to actions which produce commitment to the universal ethical values; all reinforcing each other until one reaches the ultimate resort. Allah says in the Holy Qur'an: "*As for those who believe in Allah and attach themselves to Him; He will admit them to His infinite Mercy and Grace, and He guides them unto Himself by the Straight Path.*" (An-Nisa 4:175)

صراط الذين انعمت عليهم

"(Guide us onto) the path of those on whom You have bestowed Your favor,"

The previous verse constituted a humble plea for guidance to the *Right Path*. The present verse continues that prayer and is a clarification of the *Straight Path* and a distinct specification of those who traverse it.

Ni'mah implies favor, blessings, tranquility, bliss and all that which brings about contentment. It must be acknowledged that our very being and all the amenities that facilitate our existence and development is due to the gifts and bounty of the Supreme Being, *Rabbul 'Aalameen*. It is in this regard that the Beneficent Creator makes direct reference to the innumerable universal favors bestowed on us when he says: "*If you attempt to enumerate the favors (Ni'mah) of Allah, never would you be able to calculate them.*" (Qur'an 16:18)

An'amta implies "*your particular gifts*" and refers here to the Divine bounty which is specific and perpetual. Allah has himself identified those on whom He showered His continuous Divine favor and those who qualify to receive it as being: "*Those obeying Allah and following the Prophet shall be amongst the ones on whom Allah bestowed His blessings – the Anbiyaa', Siddiqeen, Shuhadaa' and Saaliheen. What an excellent companionship that is*" (Quran 4:70). We note that there is a pointed reference to four particular categories of people:

1) *Anbiyaa' (Prophets)*

These were chosen human beings throughout history that were recipients of Divine Revelation and served as models and guides to humanity. The first of these was Adam (pbuh) and the final one is Muhammad (pbuh).

In Islam, it is an article of faith to believe in all the Divine emissaries equally, without discrimination (Q 4:152). This great and noble principle leads to the acknowledgement of the fact that all Prophets, Messengers and "Founders" of great religions were recipients of Divine Guidance and in principle, taught essentially the same ideology.

2) *Saddiqeen (Truthful)*

These are those whose very beings are cast so firmly in the mould of truthfulness that deceit, falsehood and lies find no expression in their attitude or behavior. They are genuinely true in thought, word and deed.

3) *Shuhadaa' (Martyrs)*

Those who bear testimony to truth and justice at all cost, even with their lives.

4) *Saliheen (Righteous)*

The pious ones who remain steadfast in righteousness irrespective of the circumstances surrounding them. Their Allah-consciousness evolves in them a sense of responsibility to manifest goodness and prevent evil and corruption.

When we request to be guided onto the "*Straight Path*", we ought to be fully conscious that we have to emulate the

Prophets and aspire to be like the *Siddiqeen, Shuhadaa'* and *Saaliheen*. After all, this is the Path which has been successfully trodden from the beginning of time by all those individuals and communities that have unfailingly enjoyed Allah's consistent favor and blessings.

غير المغضوب عليهم و لا الضالين

"(Let us) not (be) of those who incur Your Wrath, nor of those who go astray."

This latter portion of the final verse of the *Fatihah* makes distinct those who incur Allah's disfavour in contra-distinction to those who are referred to in *An'amta 'Alayhim*. It contains a dreadful warning about those who choose to go astray.

Two broad categories of the disfavoured are here referred to:

1) *Maghdub 'Alayhim*

These incur Allah's wrath and thereby invite Divine punishment. They violate Divine Law, their actions are not guided by sincerity and truth but are motivated by self-interest, greed, malice, and injustice. They pretend to walk on the Right Path for show or they outwardly stick to the paraphernalia of the Straight Way without the inner spirit or required consciousness or commitment.

Ghadab (subject of wrath) is here synonymous with the evil consequence a person brings upon himself by willfully rejecting or ignoring Divine Guidance and acting contrary to Divine injunctions. These are therefore appropriately subjected to the incurred wrath of the Almighty who has out of His Mercy provided them with the highest Guidance to the Straight Path.

2) *Dualleen*

Those who deliberately deviate from Divine Guidance and who due to the heedlessness, rebelliousness, immoderation, irresponsibility or arrogance lose the path and eventually wander aimlessly into the wilderness of unbelief, corruption and injustice, such forget the actual purpose of their existence and become oblivious of their moral responsibility.

Thus concludes the "*Opening Chapter*" of the Holy Qur'an, the "*Seven Oft Repeated Verses*," The "*Mother (Womb) of the Book*"; the most important Islamic prayer, *AL-FATIHAH*.

This prayer does not lead to idleress but is in fact a search for a means and thus an incentive to action. The central idea in this prayer is not for the supplicant to merely ask for certain favors but rather a humble request to be guided onto the Straight Path. A Path which is to be experienced by walking thereon in order to be successful and attain the ultimate goal.

The *Fatihah*, I reiterate, is a search for means to attain unto a higher goal via a sincere desire to actively traverse the Righteous Path.

Aamin (May it be so)!

SURAH AD – DUHA
THE MORNING LIGHT
CHAPTER 93

Early in the Prophetic Mission and after the commencement of revelation, there was suspension of revelation for a short period of time. Due to this temporary delay in Divine communication some of the Prophet's detractors scoffed at him, remarking that Allah has forgotten and forsaken him. It is during this period of difficulty and harsh taunting and reproaches of the enemies of truth that this *surah* was revealed. The flow of the *Surah* indicates that its object was to remove the anxiety and distress that the Prophet experienced. This *surah* therefore came as a stream of comfort, hope, reassurance and compassion.

The address of the entire *surah* is direct to the holy Prophet which is a special aspect, but the general lessons that we learn from the content of this *surah* is that in the trials and tribulations of life, human beings will surely experience tests; *but glad tidings to those who patiently persevere.*
(Q 2:153– 57)

و الضحى

واليل اذا سجى

"By the brightness of the morning daylight and by the night when it is overcome."

Oath

The *surah* begins with reference to natural phenomenon which symbolically refer to the brightness (of success and truth) which overcomes the darkness of (ignorance and falsehood). Just as the night and the day; light and darkness are both required, so too hardships and states of comfort in human existence. The night is eventually followed by the day, symbolically indicating that it is not proper for any person to lose hope about the appearance of light merely because of the state of darkness. Also the night and the day enforce in our psyche the lesson of contrasts as the veil of the night comes before the splendor of the daylight. Allah reminds us in Qur'an 3 verse 190 – 191 about the significance of reflecting upon the contrast in natural phenomenon by saying: *"Surely, in the creation of the heavens and the earth, in the alternation of night and day are signs for those who exercise their intellect. They are those who remember Allah whether standing, sitting or reclining and reflect upon the creation of the heavens and the earth; and exclaim (due to recognizing the reflection of the Majesty of God in creation), "O Allah you have not created all this in vain."*

ما ودعك ربك و ما قلى

"Your Lord has not forsaken you, nor is He displeased with you."

Reassurance

This verse reassures the holy Prophet that the delay in sending down revelation is not in any way on account of Allah's being displeased with him, but at the same time to bring awareness, that the entire matter of revelation is dependent on Allah's Wisdom and Will.

و للا خرة خير لك من الاولى

و لسوف يعطيك ربك فترضى

"And verily what follows will be better than what has preceded. And soon will your Lord grant you that with which you will be pleased."

Promise

Despite the temporary insults and taunts that the Prophet endured at that time, the future of his mission would be better. (Perchance, reference here is also to the Hereafter being better than this world.) When we analyze the life and struggle of this noble Prophet we witness how he started off with a small community of Believers (at the time of this revelation there were only a handful of Muslims), had to migrate from his city of birth (Makkah) but eventually overcame his enemies in various battles, starting from *Badr* when they were outnumbered 3 to 1, till the last pilgrimage when he entered his home city victorious with over a hundred thousand followers. Today, his followers are spread all over the earth and number over one billion.

As regards the Hereafter, numerous verses in the Qur'an (such as Q 9:38) clearly indicate the superiority of the permanent abode of bliss (*Jannah*) as being far more preferable than this temporary abode (*Dunya* – the temporal world).

الم يجدك يتيما فاوى
و وجدك ضالا فهدى
و وجدك عائلا فاغنى

"Did He not find you an orphan and gave you shelter. And He found you wandering and guided you. And He found you in need and enriched you."

Favors

In these verses Allah reminds the Prophet of the favorable ways Allah had opened for him. The Prophet was born after the death of his father and lost his mother six years thereafter. Yet, he had the protection of his grandfather Abdul Muttalib, then his uncle Abu Talib (may Allah reward them); employment and marriage (financial and moral support) through the first lady *Khadijah* (may Allah bless her) and a pillar of strength in his nephew, the youthful and committed 'Ali (may Allah ennoble his countenance), together with other sincere supporters.

In abstaining from the ignorant and the idolatrous practices and customs of his people, the young Muhammad (pbuh) wondered in search of ways and means to attain unto Allah. He was perplexed in his quest in finding the Creator (Q 42:53), lost in the love of God and desirous to be led to the Divine (Q12:9) and Allah guided him and made him the supreme human guide unto Him. Note that only the ignoramous would consider the word "*Daal*" to mean "astray" in the case of the holy Prophet, for the Qur'an explicitly negates the idea of the Prophet ever straying. (Q 53:2 – 3)

The great Persian poet, Sheikh Sa'di Shirazi, appropriately said about the holy Prophet, "*You reached the highest state by your perfection, you removed darkness by your beauty, beautiful are all your characteristics and achievements, salutations upon you and your family.*"

The Prophet orphaned at a very early age, poor through his youth, became the undisputed master of Arabia before his passing away and the greatest guide and benefactor to humanity. Thanks to the guidance of Allah and hail the character of the holy Prophet (pbuh).

فاما اليتيم فلا تقهر
واما السائل فلا تنهر
واما بنعمة ربك فحدث

"So, do not treat the orphan with harshness, nor refuse the one who asks and proclaim the bounty of your Lord."

Corollary to favors received

In the pervious verses mention has been made of the favors bestowed by Allah upon the Prophet and now are being mentioned the corollary to those favors. Though the address here is to the Prophet, it is also simultaneously an ordinance for the Believers in particular and humanity at large. We are instructed through the instruction to the Prophet to treat the orphans with love and respect. The Prophet (himself having been an orphan) is reported to have said, *"The best of Muslim homes is that home in which an orphan is well treated"* (Ibn Majah).

Our attention is then drawn to care for the petitioner. We all owe it as a duty to our fellow human beings to be kind, merciful, generous and helpful to those less endowed in any respect than ourselves. Though the act of begging, is not encouraged in Islam, yet the holy Prophet (pbuh) has suggested that *if a person gives up or is forced to give up his self – respect and stretches out his hand in begging such a person should not be further humiliated by being chided.*
Besides those who ask for help, there are others who do not ask though they are in desperate need. It is part of the social obligation of every worshipping person (Believer) to be conscious of the basic needs of those around them (Q 107:1 – 7). The companion Jabir narrates that: *"It never*

happened that anyone asked the Prophet for anything and he refused" (Bukhari).

The *surah* concludes by requesting that the bounties and favors of Allah be proclaimed. The greatest bounty vouchsafed to humanity is Divine Guidance and the holy Prophet, being the final recipient of Divine Guidance, is the ideal medium to communicate and announce those bounties and favors. In the Holy Qur'an, we are reminded of the fact, that *if we were to enumerate the favors and blessings of Allah, we would never be able to number them* (Qur'an 14:34).

The mode of expression and rhythm of this Surah denotes tenderness and care; containing message of affection and reassurance, generating an aura of contentment and confidence, concluding with an exhortation to manifest goodwill and proclaiming His bounties.

SURAH AL – QADR
POWER OF DIVINE REVELATION
(CHAPTER 97)

This *surah* refers to a particular event which is repeatedly celebrated by Muslims throughout the world. An event which is mentioned thrice in this short chapter. An event of great historic significance, for it marked the commencement of the Final Divine Communiqué. A communiqué that was to change the fate of nations, to cause an unparalleled change in the course of human destiny and thus have an effect, the like of which the world has never experienced before. This *surah* makes reference to the promised Great Night. The Night of Communion between this world and the Highest Existence; an event which occurred on that Night, significant for its splendor and its glory. It makes reference to the commencement of the revelation which made public the Prophetic mission of the final Divine emissary; Muhammad (pbuh).

Commencement of Revelation

انا انزلناه فى ليلة القدر

"We revealed it on 'Layla – tul – Qadr"

The Qur'an clearly refers to the commencement of Qur'anic revelation in four particular chapters of the holy Qur'an. Reference is made thrice in this *surah* to *Layla – tul – Qadr*; the Night of Power (through revelation). In Chapter 44, verse 3, we read: *"We have surely sent the Qur'an in a Blessed night."* The third reference: Chapter 2, verse 185, which declares: *"Ramadan is the month in which the Holy Qur'an was revealed as a Source of Guidance for all humanity,"* and yet in another verse, (Chapter 8 verse 43) *"If you have truly accepted faith in God and in what we have sent down to our servant on the Day of the Criterion."*

All of these references point specifically to the occasion of the initiation of the Revelation of the Holy Qur'an. The Revelation occurred in the 40th year of the life of the holy Prophet (pbuh) (610 CE) while he was meditating in the cave of *Hira*, near Makkah. He then received what is now the first five verses of Chapter 96 of the Holy Qur'an on a night designated as *Layla – tul – Qadr.*

Layla – tul – Qadr is to be sought and commemorated towards the end of *Ramadan* as the Holy Prophet (peace be upon him) said in a statement documented in *Sahih Bukhari*: *"Search for Layla – tul – Qadr in the odd nights of the last ten nights of Ramadan."*

Layla – tul – Qadr

The word *Laylah* has been used eight time in the Holy Qur'an; three times in this Chapter. It has been used in Chapter 2 verse 52, Chapter 2 verse 188, twice in Chapter 7 verse 143 and once in Chapter 44 verse 3. Wherever the word *Laylah* has been used, it has been used in connection with the revelation of the Qur'an and subjects or themes pertaining to revelation. The word *Laylah* in the present verse may signify the night which had specifically been set apart for the manifestation of Allah's special power or to a night of dignity, majesty and honor; for the Qur'anic teaching and its content is dignified, honorable and majestic. It can also imply that this *Night of Grandeur* fully meets all moral and spiritual human needs and thus renders this Final Revelation independent of any other literature or scripture. In essence, it contains basically all the essential guidance required for humanity.

When we consider the fact that a night has been chosen rather than a day for revealing the Qur'an, there seem to be a purpose for that choice. The night indicates quietness, peacefulness, tranquility. The virtuous and pious are more inclined to spend their solitude in communion with God. Thus, the night is a peaceful time, appropriate and suitable for the nourishment of the soul. In addition to the peacefulness and tranquility of the night period, the Night of *Qadr* is specifically great because the initial revelation of the Qur'an was then received on earth. The Qur'an contains an ideology, a basis for values and standards and a comprehensive code of moral and social behavior, all of which combined, promotes peace within the human soul, within society, the world at large and with the Creator.

Names and meanings

The Qur'an makes reference to this night as **Layla – tul – Qadr** in Chapter 97 and also as *Lailatul – Mubarakah* in Chapter 44. Thus it is referred to as the **Night of Power** and the **Auspicious Night**. *Layla – tul – Qadr* literally means the **Night of Decree**, the **Night of Destiny**, the **Night of Power**, the **Night of Majesty**, the **Night of Grandeur**, the **Night of Dignity**, the **Night of Ordinances**, the **Night of Determination**. All these are relevant to that great universal event of the revelation of the Qur'an. After all, it is considered the greatest and the most precious of all events which the universe has ever witnessed.

The *surah* commences after the *Basmalah* with a statement of fact that the Qur'an was revealed on the **Night of Power**, followed by a rhetorical question; which indicates an emphasis pertaining to the importance and grandeur of that night. The rhetorical question is per chance intended for us to look in retrospect, after the lapse of numerous centuries, on that glorious and magnificent event and to ponder and imagine the fascinating celebration that the spiritual world witnessed, while reflecting on the content and the essence of the revelation as a whole and its ultimate far-reaching effects on human society. By doing that, to some extent, we better appreciate why Allah says:

$$ \text{وما ادراك ما ليلة القدر} $$

"How would you know what the Night of Power really is?"

Another factor that must be born in mind is that *Layla – tul – Qadr* owes its grandeur and importance specifically to the fact that on this night the most comprehensive, perfect and of course, final of all Divine revelation was vouchsafed to the world through the agency of Gabriel to the holy Prophet Muhammad and through his family and companions to the rest of humanity.

Fasting and revelation

We also note the close association between fasting and revelation, since it was revealed in the month of *Ramadan*, as is evident from Chapter 2 verse 185 of the Holy Qur'an. We also note that Moses (pbuh) fasted 40 days prior to the reception of revelation according to <u>Exodus</u> (Chapter 24 verse 18), and that Jesus (pbuh) also fasted for 40 days before he was called upon to undertake publicly the office of Prophethood. Reference is made to this in <u>Mathew</u> (Chapter 4 verse 2). This somehow indicates that Divine blessings are

141

associated with fasting in religious history. Muslims perpetuate the tradition of Prophets and are obligated to fast in the month of *Ramadan*, the month in which the Qur'an was revealed, the month which contains *Layla – tul – Qadr*, the ninth month of the Islamic lunar calendar. We are obliged to fast the entire month every year.

ليلةالقدر خير من الف شهر

"Layla – tul – Qadr is grander than a thousand months"

A thousand months is numerically equivalent to approximately 83 years. This implies that this Night of Power is equal in worth to all other nights in a lifetime put together. It is no wonder that the holy Prophet (pbuh) is recorded to have said: *"The month of Ramadan is a blessed month. A month in which Allah has made fasting obligatory. It contains a night that is grander than a thousand months. Anyone who deprives himself of the blessing of that night truly deprives himself of tremendous blessings"* (Nasa'ie). The reference here could be to the spiritual value of the night but also for us to ascertain the gravity with which we should consider and appreciate the revelation, for its reception on earth and that particular event is more worthy than the entire life of any single human being.

Tanzil

The Qur'anic revelation (by its own account and by its very nature) is a *Tanzil* "coming down" of Divine commandment from One Who is more Majestic, Higher in Authority, Supreme. The Qur'an thus refers to itself as *Tanzil*. We therefore find reference here to the Qur'an as being,

142

تنزل الملئكة و الروح فيها باذن ربهم من كل امر

"That which the angels came down with, with frequency, by the permission of their Lord, with due command."

Tanzil also implies repetition for this Qur'an was revealed through constant revelation over a period of 23 years. The Prophet (pbuh) received the Revelation in accordance with the needs of the time, had it documented, memorized and implemented; this to remain as a Source of Guidance and Inspiration to humanity until the end of human existence in this world.

Descending of the elevated

The *Mala'ikah* and the *Ruh* which are mentioned in this verse perhaps refers to the various angels who come down in hosts accompanying Gabriel as he communicates the Divine revelation to the holy Prophet (Q 72:24 – 28). Most commentators consider *ar-Ruh* to refer specifically to the *Ruh al-Ameen*, the *trustworthy spirit* which is the title of arch angel Gabriel (Q 26:192 – 195), who is after all the Chief of Angels and of Revelation. We thus find that on the *Night of Power*, the All - Powerful, Omniscient, Omnipotent, Almighty extends His mercy of knowledge, while the angelic forces render the merciful duty of bringing forth clearly the Message, the Knowledge of Truth and the Criterion for Justice; thus fulfilling the commands of the Lord. Though revelation has ceased; in commemorating this event, we benefit spiritually from the Divine Mercy which is angelically dispensed; *"the angels descending by the permission of their Lord."*

The *clear command* also signifies that on that night every

143

matter of importance was made plain and distinct, new standards and values were established, the fortunes of generation were determined and the Criterion had been manifested.

Peace till dawn

سلام هى حتى مطلع الفجر

"Peace, till the rising of the dawn."

The word *Salaam*, here signifies complete peace; mental peace, peace of equanimity, which inspires the truthful to transcend material and sensual consideration. It implies that a conscious realization of the sanctity of this night could act as a shield against all forms of things unsavory, improper and thus one could be safeguarded and kept in peace. Those who abide by the values of what was revealed that night, should; (in this life and the Hereafter) experience tranquility, peace of mind and experience hearty satisfaction.

It is said in a *hadith* of the holy Prophet (pbuh) that angels send their salutations and peace on those who are of the 'abidin' and 'zakirin'; (*those who are in constant worship, remembering their Creator*). These angels pray for their security and ask for mercy on their behalf. We note here that peace is a distinctive mark of this night. And this peace comes to the hearts of true devotees, sincere worshippers; those who are pure in mind, in heart, in word and true in deed; such experience a special form of tranquility. The holy Prophet (pbuh) is reported to have said: *"Whosoever fasts in the holy month of Ramadan with due consideration and propriety, spends the Night of Power in worship with a pure motive of faith and devotion, will have all his/her past sins forgiven"* (Sahih Bukhari).

The state of *Peace* remains until the raising of the morning sun because it is a commemoration of that auspicious, majestic night which was the inauguration of the revelation (that has its own auspiciousness and blessings). After all, those who commemorate the grandeur of the night are recognized by the angels and noticed by the Creator. The whole night is so auspicious that it demands of us to spend most of it (at least) in adoration of the One Who sent the revelation and out of thankfulness that we are fortunate to live in that period of history where Divine revelation had reached perfection and completion.

THE VERSE OF ABUSE
OR
THE ABUSED VERSE?
AL – QUR'AN 4:34

الرجال قومون على النساء بما فضل الله
بعضهم على بعض وبما انفقوا من اموالهم
فالصالحت قانتات حافظات للغيب بما حفظ الله
و التى تخافون نشوزهن فعظوهن
واهجروهن فى المضاجع واضربوهن
فان اطعنكم فلا تبغوا عليهن سبيلا
ان الله كان عليا كبيرا.

*"Men shall take full care of women with the bounties Allah
has bestowed on them, and what they may spend out of their
possession; as Allah has eschewed each with certain
qualities in relation to the other. And the righteous women
are the truly devout ones, who guard the intimacy which
Allah has ordained to be guarded.*
*As for those woman whose ill-will you have reason to fear,
admonish them [first]; then distance yourself in bed, and
then tap them; but if they pay you heed, do not seek to harm
them. Surely, Allah is indeed the Most High, the Greatest."*

Role of family

The role of family in the overall social structure of Islam is great and if we fail to grasp its importance, the whole edifice will collapse.

In Islam there is no family without union or marriage and there is no marriage without rules and discipline. The family in Islam is a unit in which two independent persons unite and share life together. The husband's dignity is an integral part of his wife's dignity. Accordingly, neither of them is better than the other. To unite and share, there must be mutual love and compassion – a genuine feeling which; unless translated into action and behavior, would be mere illusion.

Women's rights in the family

From the very outset, Islam has been a liberating religion that uplifted the status of women and gave them rights that were considered revolutionary 1400 years ago. In spite of this founding spirit, Muslim practices today often oppress women and deny them the equality and human dignity granted in the Qur'an. The family should be the first essential area in which women's rights have to be secured.

The question that arises is that if Islam liberated women centuries ago, then why is it that maltreatment of wives is not a rare occurrence among Muslim people? Most likely, I suspect, it comes from misinterpretations of a Qur'anic verse and of some *ahadith*.

The institution of marriage

When Allah mentions marriage or the relationship between

husband and wife in the Qur'an, He describes it as one of love, mercy, and harmony between two human beings who have entered into a mutual contract. For example, *"And among His wonders is that; He created for you mates out of your own kind, so that you may incline toward them, and He engenders love and tenderness between you; in this, behold, there are messages indeed for people who think."* (Q 20:21) And, *"It is He who has created you out of one entity, so that one might incline (with love) towards the other."* (Q 7:189)

Expression of love

According to the Qur'an, the relationship between husband and wife should be one of love, mercy and mutual understanding. Allah also commands men to treat their wives, *"And consort with your wives in a goodly manner, for if you dislike something about them, it may be well that you dislike something which Allah might yet make a source of abundant good."* (Q 4:19)

The Qur'an speaks of the intimate and close relationship of the two spouses in these words: *"They are like garments unto you as you are like garments unto them"* (Q 2:187). This verse; by using the simile of garments, has explained two basic facts. First, dress is considered to be one of the most fundamental needs of human beings in all stages of life. Second, dress covers the nakedness of human beings and hides those parts which are to be kept hidden. Every person has his weakness and frailty and does not want them to be disclosed to others.

The two sexes working together, not only cover each other's weakness and frailty, but also enhance each other's capabilitiesand help each other make up their deficiencies. Men are told to be generous and liberal in their treatment of women under all circumstances, especially when the relations between the two are not very amicable. *Surah al-Baqarah* refers to this in these words: *"And do not forget liberality between yourselves"* (Q 2:237). Even in divorce, men are enjoined to be just and fair (*Ma'ruf*) to their wives. We read these words also in *Surah al-Baqarah*: *"When you divorce women, and they fulfill the term of their waiting ('iddah), either take them back honorably on equitable terms or set them free with kindness and goodness."* (Q 2:229)

So, it is through the institution of marriage that true expression is given to what the Qur'an refers to as "love and mercy" (Q 30:21) between men and women; that men and women are like each other's garments (Q 2:187), that *"be you male or female, you are members of one another"* (Q 3:195), and that *"men and women are protectors, one of another."* (Q 9:71)

Clarifying the terms **Darajah, Qawwamun** and **Faddala**

Darajah, (*step, degree or level*) is something that is earned; acquired with responsibility.

When a level is granted to male or female on the basis of their good deeds or piety, there is no discrimination. This is demonstrated by the following Qur'anic concepts: *"Unto men a fortune from what they have earned and unto women a fortune from that which they have earned"* (Q 4:32). *"Whoever works righteously; man or woman, and has faith; verily to him/her will We give a new life, a life that is good and pure. And We will bestow on such their rewards, according to the best of their actions"* (Q 4:124). So when it comes to who has greater advantage with Allah in terms of deeds, there is no level or degree given to the male or female

149

over the other.

The *darajah* for men over women occurs in the Qur'anic verse thus; "... *And (Walahunna) women shall have right similar to the rights against them according to what is equitable. But men have a degree (of advantage) over them. Allah is Exalted in Power, Wise.*" (Q 2:228)

This verse occurs among a series of verses referring to the required period of separation before claiming a divorce. The degree of advantage refers to man's being able to individually initiate divorce, whereas a woman can seek divorce only after intervention of an authority. So the advantage is limited to the circumstances of divorce only. Why this advantage? Most likely, because it is he who is duty – bound to supports the wife and unborn baby, and the previous verses are referring to the possibility that during separation the woman may be expecting, and if so, the man needs to give due consideration to taking her back because of his responsibility towards the unborn child. Hence, he has the responsibility / decision about validating the divorce or taking his wife back. Yet, in Muslim cultures, an unrestricted value is attached to this concept of "advantage" and men generalize it to all aspects of life, claiming superiority over women.

This form of unrestricted value for all circumstances contradicts the equity established in the Qur'an, "*that each 'nafs' (man or woman) is responsible for what it earns*" (Q 4:32).

The Qur'an has emphasized the female's rights (Q 2:228) with the words "*wa lahunna*" in order to neutralize the possible impression that could be created by the previous sentence of enhancing the position of men over women. Truly, it is the wondrous and miraculous expression of the Qur'an that enables it to maintain the delicacy of the problem and at the same time solve the most complicated issues in a very noble and subtle way.

Thus, in a superb manner, the Qur'an has untied the knot of this problem by saying that while men have a degree of *darajat* (advantage) in holding the key to divorce; in the enjoyment of human rights, both men and women stand equal.

Qawwamun does not convey the sense of governorship or rule over women, but rather signifies *men's role as maintainers of women*, because they support and meet their material needs from their wealth. The *Shari'ah* has entrusted the responsibility of women's material needs to men, who are held liable for meeting all the economic needs of the family; while women are held responsible for looking after the children, their nourishment, education, training, etc. This division of the work of the household between husband and wife is based on their respective natural abilities. Fulfilling these responsibilities are the primary duties, though not exclusive, yet allowing free and full participation in all social, political and ethical activities with due propriety.

Now the concept of "**Fadl**", the verse reads; *"Men shall take full care of women with the bounties Allah has bestowed on them, and what they may spend out of their possession; as Allah has eschewed each with certain qualities in relation to the other. And the righteous women are the truly devout ones, who guard the intimacy which Allah has ordained to be guarded.*
As for those women whose ill-will you have reason to fear, admonish them [first]; then distance yourself in bed, and then tap them; but if they pay you heed, do not seek to harm them. Surely, Allah is indeed the Most High, the Greatest."
(Q 4:34)

This verse is often quoted for justifying the ruthless dominance of patriarchal males demanding obedience from their wives – to the point of disciplining them through physical punishment!

But let us analyze it with Qur'anic wisdom. Firstly, the "*fadl*" or preference is related to responsibility, so there is reciprocity between this privilege and responsibility. The fact is that it is through Allah's benevolence that he gets this "*fadl*" should make a man God-conscious. So, if he is given this authority or preferential responsibility, it is accompanied by a heavy mandate and obligation. He cannot abuse the "*fadl*". The purpose of this "*fadl*" could be attributed to the fact that a family functions harmoniously when there is leadership and authority in it, manifested through fulfilling duty and mutual co – operation.

It is wrong to conclude from this that as men (or women) have some "advantage" in one respect, they are therefore superior to the other. The right attitude should be for each sex to think that it is deficient in certain aspects, which can only be complimented by the collaboration and co-operation of the other. Therefore, each sex should regard the company of the other as essential for its perfection and healthy growth. In other words, it should never fancy such ideas as its own excellence, but should consider itself dependent upon the other for its own perfection. The Qur'an has beautifully described this relationship of the two sexes in these words: "*And among His signs is that He created for you mates from among yourselves, that you may dwell in tranquility with them, and He has put love and mercy between your (hearts). Surely in that are signs for those who reflect.*" (Q 31:21)

The issue of *NUSHUZ*

Verse 4:34 has commonly been used to Justify Wife – beating. How can this be explained?

NUSHUZ could be defined as *animosity, hostility, rebellion, ill- treatment, discord, violation of marital duties on the part of either husband or wife.* In this context, a wife's *"ill-will"* implies a *deliberate, persistent breach of her marital obligations.*

The verse of *Surah Nisa'* has attracted great attention from both within the Believing community and without: *"As regards those women on whose part you fear defiance and ill – conduct, admonish them (first), (next) separate in bed, (and last) tap them (if they still persist in their defiance); but if they cooperate and pay you heed, do not look for excuses to harm them. Note well that there is Allah above you all."* (Q 4:34)

In the context of the above verse the most appropriate meaning for *nushuz* is *marital discord (ill – will, animosity etc.)*. The process suggested is necessary, otherwise it is inviting the likelihood of divorce without any reconciliation procedure and this will contravene the Qur'anic guidance. The separation could be temporary or permanent depending on the reconciliation procedure, and this fits in very well with the divorce procedure outlined in the Qur'an (see 8.5). Therefore the more accurate understanding of the above verse would be: (4:34) *"... As for those women whose animosity or ill – will you have reason to fear, discuss the matter with them, then separate in bed, then tap; and if they pay you heed, do not seek a way against them."*

The verse following the above verse gives further weight to the above translation. (4:35) *"And if you fear a breach between them (the man and the wife), appoint an arbiter from his folk and an arbiter from her folk. If they desire amendment, Allah will make them one of mind. Lo! Allah is Ever Knower, Aware."*

An added weight to the meanings outlined above is given by verse (4:128), where in the case of man the same word, *nushuz*, is also used. Note too that as ill – treatment emanating here is from the husband, a process of reconciliation is encouraged!
"If a wife fears ill – treatment (nushuz) or desertion (i'raad) on her husband's part, there is no blame on them if they arrange an amicable settlement between themselves; and such settlement is best..." (Q 4:128)

In the same *surah* we read, *"Whoever among you; men or women, are guilty of this crime (impropriety / obscenity), punish them both; then if they both repent and reform themselves, leave them alone, for Allah is Most Generous in accepting repentance, and Merciful in forgiving sins."* (4:16)

As previously mentioned, women could only be taken to task when they were guilty of open obscenity. The verse (Q 4:16) clearly states that whoever commits open licentiousness, man or woman, must be punished. It may here be mentioned that this open obscenity or licentiousness (*nushuz*) means obscenity short of adultery and fornication.

If a wife fears that her husband is going to be excessive, there is the same process for the wife too. She can advise him first. Psychological pressure of withdrawing closeness and intimacy? But why is there no reference to physical pressure,

154

like a symbolic slap or the like? The wife is not required to slap her husband, guarding against the possibility of physical retaliation and its dire consequences. But she has use of an injunction, which is better than that; to sit down with respected members of the community, (if need be with a judge), and draw up a contract with the man, which says: *You have done this or that – if you do it again, this will be the consequences.* In other words, she is getting the community behind her.

Three steps for regaining marital harmony or an amicable settlement

We note that in the event that there is a disruption of marital harmony, the Qur'an suggest three steps for regaining harmony. In order of preference, they are:
(Step1) *Wa'z* (admonition, consultation and discussion). This is the preferred method suggested for regaining marital harmony and is the same mechanism discussed in the Qur'an for the coordination of affairs between ali groups of people. Consultation can be between the parties (as in 4:34) or between the two parties with the help of arbiters or *hakim* (4:35, 4:128). *Wa'z* or *admonition* implies advising and reminding one of the consequence of one's actions; this, in a way that softens the heart of the listener (16:125) and making him / her incline favorably to your words.

(Step 2) *Wahjur* (to separate in bed; time and space boycott, at least one night). If consultation does not lead to marital harmony, the second suggestion of time-out, a phrase to denote a separation in time and /or space between two people. This is a form of psychological pressure. Note that it is avoidance in the bed itself and not avoidance from the bed. Furthermore, it is avoidance in the bed and not avoidance in the house or in front of the family, children and so forth.

155

The purpose of that act is to solve the problem well – known, not to belittle the woman or uncover the secretes that are going on. However, it is a reaction to her act of *nushooz* and recalcitrance by avoiding her and turning away from her in hope that this will lead to reciprocity and togetherness. It can be for an intermediate cooling off period only, or could presumably continue indefinitely, which in the context of marriage could only mean divorce.

(Step 3) ***Daraba*** (a gentle strike or tap; an expression of physical pressure.) If the first two methods are used in their preferred order to the fullest extent, the need for the third method of a strike would not be reached.

A famous Multi – meaning word *"Daraba"*

The problem of abuse comes from the word *"Idribuhunne"* which is usually translated as *"beat them"*. The root of this word is *"Daraba"*. If one consults any Arabic dictionary you would find a long list of meanings ascribed to this word!

The list is one of the longest lists in the whole Arabic dictionaries and has so many different meanings. In the Qur'an, depending on the context, one can ascribe different meanings to it. ie.:

To travel, to get out: 3:156; 4:101; 38:44; 73:20; 1:273

To strike: 2:60,70; 7:160; 8:12; 20:77; 24:31; 26:63; 37:93; 47:04

To beat: 8:50; 47:27

To set up: 43:58; 57:13

To give (examples): 14:24 – 45; 16:75,76,112; 18:32,45; 24:35; 30:28,58; 36:78;
39:27,29; 43:17; 59:21; 66:10 – 11

To take away, to ignore: 43:5

To condemn: 2:61
To seal, to draw over: 18:11
To cover: 24:31
To explain: 13:17

Thus, in the Qur'an alone we witness the verb *"Daraba"* having at least ten different meanings. *"Daraba"* has also other meanings which are not mentioned in the Qur'an. For example, in the Arabic language, you do not print money- - you *"Daraba"* money, you do not multiply numbers- -you *"Daraba"* numbers, you do not cease the work- - you *"Daraba"* the work –

Webster's dictionary gives fourteen meanings to the verb **"strike"**: hit (against); ignite; (of snake) bite; (of plants) (cause to) take root; attack; hook (fish); sound (time) as bell in clock; affect; arrive at, come upon; enter mind of; discover (gold, oil etc.); dismantle' remove; make (coin); cease work as protest or to make demands. The same dictionary gives eight meanings to the verb "beat": strike repeatedly; overcome; surpass; stir vigorously with striking action; flap (wings); make, wear (path); throb; sail against wind.

When we encounter a multi – meaning word, we select the proper meaning according to the context, form and common sense.

Why the *"daraba"*?

Why has the Qur'an included the method of a "strike"? The Qur'an always emphasizes doing good and abstaining from evil. If the Qur'an is looked at as an integrated and cohesive text, situations can be identified where the Qur'an calls for the

157

prohibition of certain things in stages. For example, whereas early revelations discourage the use of intoxicants (2:219, 4:43), the final revelation on this matter clearly condemns and prohibits them (5:93 – 94).

This is where there is a need to understand the historical context in which the Qur'an was revealed. It is known that in the pre-Islamic period known as the Age of Ignorance (*Jahiliyyah*), there were gross practices of physical and emotional abuse of females such as female infanticide (killing of babies) and the custom of inheriting the wives of deceased relatives against the will of the women. Verse 4:34, which refers to a strike / tap was revealed early in the Medinan period at a time when cruelty and violence against women were still rampant. Seen within this context the strike is a restriction on existing practice, and not a recommendation. As Muslim society in Madinah developed towards an ideal state, the final verse in the Qur'an on male – female relationship (9:71) regards women and men as being each other's protecting friends and guardians (*'awliyya*) which emphasizes their cooperation in living together as partners.

In addition, this spirit can be used in viewing the *Hadith* and classical commentaries by Muslim jurists on the strike or *daraba*. *Ahadith* on *striking in such a way as not to cause pain (ghayr mubarrih)* are reported by Muslim, Tirmidhi, Abu Daud, Nasa'ie and Ibn Majah. The authorities stress that *if a strike is resorted to, it should be merely symbolic such as a strike with a toothbrush or folded handkerchief* (Tabari and Razi). Imam Shaf'ie is of the opinion *that striking should preferably be avoided completely.*

It can thus be concluded that the call for the (single) strike is a restriction and not a recommendation; as when the first two steps are practiced effectively, there is no need for a third step.

Obedience misconstrued

The Qur'an does not order women to slavishly obey their husbands. It says *good women are qanitat (have qunut)*. *Qunut* is used for both women and men (3:17, 33:35) and non – humans (39:9, 2:117). *Qunut* does not refer to the obedience of a wife to a husband or of any human to another. It refers to the spirit of humility before Allah. When the verse goes on to say "if they obey you," the Qur'an uses the term *ta'a*, which means for one human to follow the orders of another, referring not just to women obeying men, but men following orders as well (4:59). *Ta'a* is not used here in the command form for women, rather the Qur'an places a firm admonishment on the men: "*If they (female) pay you heed (male)*" the males are commanded "*not to seek a way against (the women)*". "*If they obey you*" does not mean that women have an obligation to slavishly obey men. Nor does it mean that if a woman disobeys, a husband can beat her. The focus is on the responsibility of men to treat women fairly, especially when women follow their suggestions.

Most of the women beaten nowadays are not beaten because the first two conditions have been met with, but are in fact, beaten because of the husband's anger over some petty issue. Such behavior is not that of a sincere Muslim and obviously has no sanction in the Qur'an whatsoever.

It is evident from many authentic traditions that the Prophet himself intensely detested the idea of beating one's wife, and said on more than one occasion, "*Could anyone of you beat his wife as if she is a slave, and then lie with her in the evening?*" (Bukhari and Muslim). According to another

159

tradition, he forbade the beating of any woman with the words, *"Never beat God's handmaidens"* (Abu Daud, Ibn Majah, Ahmad Ibn Hanbal, Ibn Hibban and Hakim, on the authority of Iyas ibn 'Abd Allah; Ibn Hibban, on the authority of 'Abd Allah Ibn Abbas; and Bayhaqi on the authority of Umm Kulthum).

Next to piety, the believer finds nothing better for him than a virtuous wife. If he bids her good, she obeys. If he looks at her she gives him pleasure. If she gives him a promise, she fulfills it. If he is absent from her, she guards herself and his property. (Ibn Majah)
This *hadith* states that the wife should obey her husband, but to what extent? Obviously, she cannot obey her husband in anything that is *haram*. Not only that, but the obedience of the wife is in those duties listed above, viz. ... with regard to cohabitation, domestic matters, guarding his property, and not allowing others to violate her / his dignity or their belongings.

In summary, there is the following *hadith* from the Prophet on the rights of a wife. A person asked the Messenger of Allah, *"What rights does the wife of one among us have over him?"* His answer was, *"It is that you shall give her food, you shall not slap her on the face, nor revile her, nor leave her alone except within the house"* (Ahmad, Abu Da'ud, Ibn Majah). This implies provision, residence, respect and security.

Appreciation

Some husbands get upset when their wives refuse to do this or that around the house. This has subjected many wives to physical mistreatment. But the following incident clearly shows that it is not the duty of the wife to tend after the house, and therefore, it can in no way justify any sort of retort on the part of the husband. In fact, the following quote would make it seem that many women nowadays should be the one's complaining as they are forced to do work that they are not truly totally responsible for:

It is reported that a man once came to 'Umar, the second Caliph, with the intention of bringing to his notice certain complaints he had against his wife. When he reached the door of 'Umar's house, he heard the Caliph's wife railing against him. Hearing this he went back as he thought that the Caliph himself was in the same predicament and could therefore hardly be expected to set matters right for him. 'Umar coming out of his house, saw the person going back. So he called him back and inquired as to the purpose, which had brought him to his house. He said that he had come to him with some complaints against his wife, but turned back on finding that the Caliph himself was subject to the same treatment from his wife. 'Umar said to him that the patiently bore the excesses of his wife because she had certain rights over him. *"Is it not true that she cooks my food, washes my clothes and suckles my children, thus relieving me of the necessity of employing a cook, a washerman and a nurse, although she is not in the slightest degree responsible for this? Not only that, I enjoy peace of mind on account of her and I am protected from committing the sin of adultery. In view of these advantages, I put up with her excesses. You should also do the same."*

Having clarified some of the misconceptions, countered some distortions, we acknowledge, of course, that not all men or women are following the teachings of the Qur'an in their relationships. Rather than looking at the verse holistically, they only focus on it with a bias to their advantage and abuse it. Men exploit and women rebel. Where men have done so, and women have remained ignorant, injustices have taken place even to the point of physical abuse. Some women, in their ignorance on the issue, have taken this as their Islamic plight. So, for their own benefit, women need to acquire knowledge from the Qur'an, become more aware, rally around it and assert themselves for fairness and justice.

Men should also understand the Qur'an with a fair and just mind without cultural filters and communicate with each other about it so that they can strive together for betterment in their spiritual path.

Prophetic Example

The *Hadith*, which we must realize is a record of the sayings and doings of the Prophet (pbuh), and the second source of Muslim law and practice, records the Prophet (pbuh) as saying: *"The best of you is he who is best to his wife."* Aishah (RA) narrates that the holy *Prophet never hit a servant or a woman.*

The demeanor of the Messenger (pbuh) toward women, his attitude toward conflict resolution among couples, his exemplary treatment of his wives, his practice of gender – neutral consultation, his abhorrence of violence towards women, his love for all and his persistent efforts to alleviate the human condition; all bring us to the conclusion that he wanted to usher in freedom, dignity and equality; making everyone conscious of only one God – the God of all humans beings, not a chauvinistic God.

The Qur'an does not discriminate between the two sexes in any way that undermines their full worth as equal human beings, nor does it give either of them; men or women, priority or superiority over the other in any manner whatsoever, neither does it endorse spouse abuse nor does it encourage spouse battering. Just as men have rights over women, likewise women have rights over men. Just as women have certain duties and obligations, likewise men have certain duties and obligations.

Research has shown that oppressive interpretations of the Qur'an are influenced mostly by cultural practices and values which regard women as inferior and subordinate to men. It is not Islam that oppress women, but human beings that have failed to understand Allah's directives.

The honor or superiority of any person cannot be established on the basis of color, race, nationality, gender or family. It must be judged on the basis of his or her piety, conduct and excellence of character, which must be good and virtuous in word and deed. The more a person is good and virtuous in word and action, the greater is his/ her excellence; *"Surely, the most honored of you in the sight of Allah is the pious, the most righteous"* (49:13).

GLOSSARY

Allah	The proper name of the Supreme Being Who exists necessarily by Himself. This word comprises all the attributes of perfection.
Ayah	Sign, verse of the Holy Qur'an
Deen	Religion, judgement, way of life. Islam is called 'Al-Deen', the way of life, as it is not a religion of rituals but a complete way of life including spiritual, social, economical and political systems providing guidance for private, public, national and international issues.
Hajj	The obligatory pilgrimage to Makkah during the lunar month of *Zul-Hajj*.
Ilah	Object of worship
Jinn	A definite order of conscious being, intelligent, corporeal and usually invisible, made of smokeless flame.
Juz'	One of the thirty parts of the Qur'an
Ka'bah	This term is used for a cube shaped building in the center of the Sacred Mosque in Makkah.
Salaah	Obligatory prayer in the prescribed form, offered five times a day at prescribed times.

Shirk	A combination of idolatry, heathenism, polytheism, paganism, egoism, etc.
Sunnah	Dispensation, tradition, way of doing things and also the traditions and the actions of the Prophet Muhammad (pbuh).
Surah	A chapter of the Qur'an.